5 STEPS TO A 5™

500

AP World History Questions
to know by test day

SECOND EDITION

Adam Stevens

Sean McManamon

Mc Graw Hill Education

New York Chicago San Francisco Athens London Madrid
Mexico City Milan New Delhi Singapore Sydney Toronto

1 2 3 4 5 6 7 8 9   QFR   21 20 19 18 17 16

ISBN   978-1-259-83675-6
MHID   1-259-83675-4

e-ISBN   978-1-259-83676-3
e-MHID   1-259-83676-2

CONTENTS

ABOUT THE AUTHORS

Adam Stevens graduated from Columbia University with a BA in history in 1996 and has taught history in Brooklyn public high schools since then. He lives in Brooklyn with his wife, Helena, and is lucky to have three wonderful children, Omar, Alex and Iliana.

Sean McManamon has a Masters in History from Hunter College, 1998. He teaches AP World History at Brooklyn Technical High School and lives in Manhattan with his wife, Justine, and two children, Phebe and Owen.

INTRODUCTION

Congratulations! You've taken a big step toward AP success by purchasing *5 Steps to a 5: 500 AP World History Questions to Know by Test Day*. We are here to help you take the next step and score high on your AP Exam so you can earn college credits and get into the college or university of your choice!

This book gives you 500 AP-style multiple-choice questions that cover all the most essential course material. Each question has a detailed answer explanation. These questions will give you valuable independent practice to supplement your regular textbook and the groundwork you are already doing in your AP classroom.

Each chapter ends with a set of stimulus-based questions of the type the College Board has recently employed in its re-designed AP World History exam. As you complete these questions use a timer, and work toward completing each stimulus-based question in one minute or less. Working at this speed will prepare you for the pace you will want to maintain when taking the actual AP exam in the spring.

This and the other books in this series were written by expert AP teachers who know your exam inside out and can identify the crucial exam information as well as questions that are most likely to appear on the exam.

You might be the kind of student who takes several AP courses and needs to study extra questions a few weeks before the exam for a final review. Or you might be the kind of student who puts off preparing until the last weeks before the exam. No matter what your preparation style, you will surely benefit from reviewing these 500 questions, which closely parallel the content, format, and degree of difficulty of the questions on the actual AP exam. These questions and their answer explanations are the ideal last-minute study tool for those final few weeks before the test.

Remember the old saying "Practice makes perfect." If you practice with all the questions and answers in this book, we are certain you will build the skills and confidence needed to do great on the exam. Good luck!

—Editors of McGraw-Hill Education

5 STEPS TO A 5™

500
AP World History Questions
to know by test day

CHAPTER 1

Foundations: 8000 BCE to 600 CE

Controlling Idea

In the Foundations unit basic patterns of human interaction that we adhere to in today's world arise. For the first time, with the origins of agriculture, humans were able to consistently generate food on a scale beyond what was needed by the individual producer to survive. This surplus production, and various social and political arrangements constructed to regulate its distribution in human populations, is the fundamental point of departure in AP World History. Class society, a society of laborers and owners (with diverse subdivisions of these two major groups), emerged in each center of civilization and shaped how this surplus was to be shared. The move to ownership disproportionately enriched males and so we see the origins of patriarchy in the Foundations era as well. Finally, religions and belief systems that shape the worldviews of billions today can be traced to this period of history, the Foundations era.

1. Which of the following was NOT a common trait of early civilizations?
   (A) Writing
   (B) Formal state structures
   (C) Urban life
   (D) Nomadism

2. Where did the earliest civilizations tend to develop?
   (A) Mountain plateaus
   (B) Coastlines
   (C) River valleys
   (D) Grassland steppes

3. Based on the preponderance of archaeological evidence, which region of the world saw the development of the earliest civilizations?

(A) Northern Eurasia
(B) South America
(C) Indonesia
(D) The Middle East

4. Which people are generally credited with founding Mesopotamian civilization in the Tigris-Euphrates river valley?

(A) Akkadians
(B) Hittites
(C) Sumerians
(D) Greeks

5. What conclusions can we draw about Babylonian society from the following excerpt from Hammurabi's Code?

221. If a physician heals the broken bone or diseased soft part of a man, the patient shall pay the physician five shekels in money. 222. If he were a freed man he shall pay three shekels. 223. If he were a slave his owner shall pay the physician two shekels.

(A) Babylonian medical practice was informed by study of microscopic germs.
(B) Babylonian physicians attended formal medical school for many years of training similar to doctors today.
(C) Babylonian physicians healed most cases of broken bones in Mesopotamia.
(D) Babylonian medical practice reflected prevailing patterns in social status.

6. Which of the following is NOT true of the ancient Egyptian pyramids?

(A) Served as tombs for pharaohs
(B) Were built by slave and corvee labor
(C) Are reflective of advanced geometric knowledge
(D) Were built under the influence of Chinese advisors

7. Which of the following early river valley civilizations developed in the greatest state of isolation from the others?

(A) Tigris River
(B) Euphrates River
(C) Indus River
(D) Huang He River

8. Which people are credited with developing the first phonetic alphabet?

(A) Egyptians
(B) Sumerians
(C) Phoenicians
(D) Chinese

9. Which choice best characterizes the relationship between early civilizations and writing?

(A) Writing permitted record keeping for trade and governments.
(B) Writing led to the development of civilization more than sedentary agriculture.
(C) Most civilizations developed without writing systems.
(D) No sophisticated civilization developed without a system of writing.

10. Which of the following was true for ALL of the early agricultural systems?

(A) Domestication of perennial plants in each region
(B) Wheat and barley cultivation
(C) Economic activity based on raising a combination of domesticated plants and draft animals
(D) Primary reliance on pastoral forms of social organization

11. Which statement is most accurate regarding Jewish monotheism?

(A) It traces its origins to Abraham.
(B) It was spread by missionaries in the Ganges River valley.
(C) It appealed mainly to wealthier people.
(D) It incorporated the idea of reincarnation.

12. Confucianism, Hinduism, and Christianity had what in common?

(A) They directed attention to the afterlife.
(B) They helped justify and preserve social inequality.
(C) They urged the importance of political activity.
(D) They stressed the value of warfare.

13. Which of the following did ancient Egyptian, Shang, and Sumerian civilizations all have in common?

(A) Pyramid-shaped monumental architecture
(B) River valley location
(C) Acceptance of Buddhism
(D) Pastoral-based economy

14. The period 8000 BCE to 600 CE saw all of the following EXCEPT

(A) Birth of major world religions
(B) Origin of agriculture
(C) Use of gunpowder
(D) Urbanization

15. Which of the following classical societies was based in the eastern Mediterranean Sea?

(A) Greek
(B) Mauryan
(C) Han
(D) Gupta

16. River valley civilizations, such as the Egyptians or Sumerians, developed all of the following EXCEPT

(A) Craft specialization
(B) Social stratification
(C) Constitutional monarchy
(D) Long-distance trade

17. Which ancient civilization fits the description found below?

- Constructed multistory structures
- Arose near the Indus River
- Disappeared for reasons that remain unclear

(A) Harappan
(B) Shang
(C) Kushite
(D) Mayan

18. Which civilization's decline was most likely due to drastic environmental change?

(A) Indus
(B) Han
(C) Roman
(D) Egyptian

19. Which example from the classical world best characterizes the principle of cultural diffusion?

(A) Preference for silk garments among the Roman elite
(B) Victory of Sparta in the Peloponnesian War
(C) Conversion of Asoka to Buddhism
(D) Growing influence of Confucianism in China during the Han dynasty

20. All of the following were important impacts of the rise of metalwork in the ancient world EXCEPT:

(A) Metal tools make farming easier.

(B) Metal arms revolutionized war fighting.

(C) Specialized labor developed further.

(D) Metal ships revolutionized trade and naval warfare.

21. What additional challenge do historians studying the Harappan civilization of the Indus River valley face that does not exist when studying Sumerian or Egyptian civilizations?

(A) Artifacts lie under layers of earth that must be carefully excavated by archaeologists.

(B) Religious prohibitions on interfering with the burial places of the Hindu dead slow excavation projects.

(C) Historians rely entirely on legends and oral history as no archaeological record of Harappan civilization exists.

(D) Harappan writing has never been deciphered.

22. Which is the name of the ancient Sumerian writing system?

(A) Hieroglyphics

(B) Ideograph

(C) Pictograph

(D) Cuneiform

23. The order in which these empires or civilizations emerged was

　I. Sumerian

　II. Shang

　III. Roman

　IV. Han

(A) I, II, III, IV

(B) I, II, IV, III

(C) II, I, IV, III

(D) II, III, I, IV

24. Based on available knowledge, which of the following was NOT a part of *Homo erectus'* world?

(A) Tool making

(B) Language

(C) Bipedalism

(D) Agriculture

25. Compared to other revolutions in world history, which feature of the Neolithic Revolution is most unusual?

(A) Altered gender roles and relations
(B) Attenuated unfolding over thousands of years in diverse locales
(C) Impact on population growth
(D) Transformation of class relations

26. Which set of Paleolithic practices would prove most durable as humans entered the Neolithic era?

(A) Generally egalitarian principles of social organization
(B) Metallurgical expertise
(C) Domestication of animals
(D) Nomadic lifestyle

27. Which of the following was NOT a unique advantage agricultural people enjoyed over hunter-gatherer groups as a sedentary lifestyle began to confront nomadic lifestyles after 8000 BCE?

(A) Immunities built up to new diseases spawned in denser nodes of population
(B) Regular armed forces capable of sustained offensive and defensive campaigns
(C) Greater ability to store food in preparation for times of scarcity
(D) Higher levels of social equality and group cohesion

28. In what respects did pastoralism lay important foundations for subsequent stages of human development?

(A) Human societies first began to follow the leadership of recognized spiritual guides.
(B) Domesticated mammals began to provide more consistent sources of hides, bone, and protein.
(C) Groups learned how to select seeds and grains that over time yielded more bountiful harvests.
(D) Settled living formed the basis for early writing systems.

29. Which of the following early crops was unique to the early civilizations of what would later be termed the New World?

(A) Oats
(B) Millet
(C) Barley
(D) Maize

30. What best characterizes the evolving role of women as human society moved from preagricultural to agricultural modes of production?

(A) Tending to large flocks of domesticated animals

(B) Foraging and fashioning stone tools

(C) Having greater confinement to the home to care for more numerous children

(D) Spending most time at the market to trade the family's surplus farm goods

31. Which of the following best describes the development of agriculture during the Neolithic era?

(A) It was a gradual process, arising independently in diverse regions and climatic conditions on the globe.

(B) It spread from the Americas across a land bridge to Asia and then to Europe.

(C) It was limited to China until the first millennium BCE.

(D) It was practiced only on hilly terrain.

32. What economic effect did food surpluses have on early agricultural societies?

(A) Hunting animals was eliminated as a source of food.

(B) A social hierarchy developed with peasants on the top.

(C) The first long-distance trade networks were established.

(D) Trade practices emerged with the capacity to feed artisans who then had time to practice craft specialization.

33. What, in general, was the health impact as human populations abandoned nomadism and settled into a sedentary agricultural lifestyle?

(A) Rates of parasitic diseases were reduced.

(B) Greater exposure to pathogens due to proximity to farm animals and human waste caused new sicknesses.

(C) Disease rates fell due to the vigorous lifestyle of hard labor.

(D) Nutrition generally improved, resulting from the greater diversity of foodstuffs the laboring peasantry had to choose from.

34. Which of the following is associated with the "Out of Africa" thesis on human origins?
    I. Origin of anatomically modern humans in Africa
    II. Separate origins of anatomically modern humans across the Old World
    III. Evolution of *Homo neanderthalensis* into *Homo sapiens*
    (A) I and III
    (B) II only
    (C) II and III
    (D) I only

35. Broadly speaking, which choice places the developments associated with the Neolithic Revolution in the correct chronological order?
    (A) Specialization of labor, social stratification, surplus food production
    (B) Surplus food production, specialization of labor, social stratification
    (C) Social stratification, specialization of labor, surplus food production
    (D) Specialization of labor, surplus food production, social stratification

36. Which of the following is the least intensive and sophisticated agricultural practice?
    (A) Use of chemical fertilizer
    (B) Irrigation
    (C) Terrace farming
    (D) Slash and burn

37. The preponderance of evidence would suggest that human settlement reached which of the following regions most recently?
    (A) Australia
    (B) South America
    (C) Scandinavia
    (D) India

38. Which region of the world had yet to experience the Neolithic transition by 600 CE?
    (A) Mesoamerica
    (B) South America
    (C) Northern Europe
    (D) Australia

39. The label "Paleolithic" sometimes serves as a substitute for which of the following?
    I. Bronze Age
    II. Iron Age
    III. Stone Age

    (A) I and II
    (B) II and III
    (C) I and III
    (D) III only

40. Hellenistic culture epitomizes which of the following historical forces or trends?

    (A) Isolationism
    (B) Cultural diffusion
    (C) Patriarchy
    (D) Egalitarianism

41. Hellenistic culture brought together the traditions of which of the following regions?

    (A) Mediterranean, Mesoamerican, sub-Saharan African
    (B) Middle Eastern, Mediterranean, Scandinavian
    (C) Mesoamerican, Scandinavian, Mediterranean
    (D) Middle Eastern, Mediterranean, South Asian

42. Which of the following political practices remained continuous from the period of the Republic into the period of the Roman Empire?

    (A) Strict rules separating military service and political leadership
    (B) Dominant involvement of the plebian classes in state affairs
    (C) Primacy placed in a Senate where state affairs were debated
    (D) Recruitment of local elites in recently conquered areas to represent the interests of the imperial center

43. Which of the following prominent Greeks exercised practical political leadership?

    (A) Aristotle
    (B) Solon
    (C) Plato
    (D) Socrates

44. Which choice best describes the position of women in classical Athens in terms of divorce and property rights as compared to women in classical Roman society? Greek women had

    (A) Far greater rights
    (B) Somewhat greater rights
    (C) About the same level of rights
    (D) Far fewer rights

45. Which of the following pairings most accurately reflects existing trade connections in the Greco-Roman era?

    (A) Han-Roman
    (B) Scandinavian-Greek
    (C) Polynesian-Roman
    (D) Gupta-Greek

46. Which prominent Greek individual listed below was not part of a direct teacher-student relationship shared by the other four?

    (A) Alexander the Great
    (B) Socrates
    (C) Aristotle
    (D) Herodotus

47. Which of the following best describes BOTH the Roman and the Han empires?

    (A) Neither empire was linked to the Silk Roads.
    (B) Both empires used the family as the model for state organization.
    (C) Mounting costs associated with defending imperial frontiers led to economic and political crises.
    (D) New religions were easily assimilated into existing imperial religious ideologies.

48. What was a common feature of classical civilizations in India, China, and the Mediterranean?

    (A) Agricultural systems dependent on monsoon rains
    (B) Social hierarchy
    (C) Absence of coerced labor
    (D) Elimination of patriarchy over time

49. What similarity did early Buddhism and early Christianity share?

    (A) Support for caste hierarchy
    (B) Requirement of total celibacy for men
    (C) Allowance of women to enter monastic life
    (D) Inclusion of Greek and Roman gods into their pantheon

50. Which pair of rulers underwent a religious conversion process that had a broad-based impact on the lands under their control?

    (A) Julius Caesar and Shi Huangdi
    (B) Hammurabi and Julius Caesar
    (C) Tutankhamen and Pericles
    (D) Asoka and Constantine

51. Which policy did both Roman and Han armies tend to implement upon taking control of a foreign land?

    (A) Enslavement of the entire working-age population
    (B) Repression of local worship and imposition of a state religion
    (C) Cessation of trade contact with the rest of the world
    (D) Relative autonomy for cooperative local elites

52. Before 600 CE, nomadic peoples of the Eurasian landmass

    (A) Lived in a state of constant warfare with neighboring civilizations
    (B) Were dependent on the camel for covering large distances
    (C) Maintained strict isolation from nearby civilizations
    (D) Interacted intermittently with civilizations, often through trade

53. Why did the western portion of the Roman Empire suffer so much more in the breakdown of Roman imperial unity than the regions of the Eastern Roman Empire (Byzantium)?

    (A) The feudal system in the west relied on a trade system made unreliable by harsh winters.
    (B) The Eastern Roman world had traditionally been more economically vibrant due to more active trade links with the East.
    (C) Popes of the Roman Catholic church maintained harmonious relations with western feudal lords.
    (D) The Eastern Orthodox church attracted more followers than the Roman church.

54. Which of the following is the most accurate statement about ancient Roman trade routes?

(A) On every trade route enslaved persons were the chief commodity being transported.

(B) Western Europe was the most profitable trade destination of the empire and had the most trade routes.

(C) Most trade routes were focused around the Mediterranean Sea.

(D) The Silk Road was Rome's most important trade route.

55. Which weakness of the Roman Empire contributed most directly to its collapse?

(A) It was too vast to impose unity and order among all of the regions.

(B) Mountain ranges blocked effective transport and communications between key areas.

(C) It was too small to marshal resources necessary to protect itself from rival powers.

(D) Repeated incursions into the territories of powerful empires to the east resulted in devastating offensives.

56. After the fall of Rome, the eastern half of the empire became renamed the

(A) Holy Roman Empire

(B) Bactrian Empire

(C) Byzantine Empire

(D) Visigoth Kingdom

57. Which of the following civilizations afforded the greatest degree of citizen input into government policy?

(A) Han

(B) Roman

(C) Sumerian

(D) Egyptian

58. In Greek civilization, women

(A) Held slave status in every household

(B) Enjoyed political equality with men

(C) Were afforded the same rights no matter the city-state in which they happened to reside

(D) Were considered inferior to men in both the private and public spheres

59. Christianity's rise is most accurately viewed as a modification of which of the following?

(A) Islam
(B) Hinduism
(C) Judaism
(D) Confucianism

60. Which of the following terms is NOT associated with classical Greek architecture?

(A) Doric
(B) Ionic
(C) Corinthian
(D) Ziggurat

61. Which neighboring power posed the greatest military threat over the course of classical Greek civilization?

(A) Egyptian
(B) Mongol
(C) Persian
(D) Balkan

62. The geographic factors presented here led to the development of which highly complex and distinctive civilization by the year 600 CE?

- Fertile river valleys
- Isolating mountain ranges
- Dependable monsoon weather patterns

(A) Indian
(B) Roman
(C) Mayan
(D) Sumerian

63. Which of the following best describes political patterns on the Indian subcontinent in the classical era 1000 BCE to 600 CE?

(A) Stateless societies
(B) Continuous dynastic rule under the Maurya Empire
(C) Decentralized rule by local princes lacking any form of subcontinent-wide authority at any point
(D) Decentralized rule by local princes punctuated by Maurya and Gupta periods of unification

64. Which was the most effective unifying force in early Indian culture?
    (A) Long-distance trade with East Asian civilizations
    (B) Widely practiced and similar Hindu tradition, including the caste system
    (C) Expansion of Buddhist influence
    (D) Recognized central political authority

65. Which of the following is unique to the Hindu religion when compared to other major world religions?
    I. Belief in some form of afterlife
    II. Absence of a central founding figure
    III. Distinct denominations
    (A) I only
    (B) II only
    (C) I and II
    (D) II and III

66. Which major world religion lacks a central founding figure?
    (A) Christianity
    (B) Islam
    (C) Judaism
    (D) Hinduism

67. Which is NOT a significant continuity Buddhism carried over from its Hindu roots?
    (A) Endorsement of caste stratification
    (B) Belief in an afterlife
    (C) Concern with and reverence for beauty in nature
    (D) Ornate temple architecture

68. How did the Hindu doctrine of dharma impact Indian society?
    (A) It fostered the formation of rigid social and economic groups.
    (B) It was the basis of equality under the law between men and women.
    (C) It influenced the priestly class to implement a standardized set of religious rituals for Hindus.
    (D) It initiated an integrated economic system to aid merchants.

69. Which of the following ancient texts did not serve as a spiritual guide to salvation for those who lived by it?

(A) Vedas
(B) Analects
(C) Torah
(D) New Testament of the Bible

70. Which important idea is credited to intellectuals of the Gupta Empire?

(A) Invention of the telescope
(B) Development of humanity's first written script
(C) The concept of zero
(D) Invention of the magnetic compass

71. Which beliefs do Hinduism and Buddhism have in common?

(A) Belief in the caste system
(B) Damnation for sinners
(C) Reverence for Muhammad
(D) Reincarnation

72. Which lasting pattern in the history of the subcontinent can we trace to the period of the rule of the Maurya and Gupta empires in India?

(A) Strong state sponsorship of Hindu beliefs
(B) Invasion and rule by nomadic invaders
(C) Difficulty in maintaining centralized imperial rule
(D) Long and generally unbroken eras of centralized imperial rule

73. Why did long-distance trade flourish in the classical world?

(A) Stable imperial authority provided safe passage for merchants.
(B) Circumnavigation of the globe by the Romans increased access to goods from distant lands.
(C) Silk Roads were so safe that individual traders frequently traveled their entire distance.
(D) Stable central rule in India throughout the period made it a vital hub of trade.

74. Buddhism's rise is most accurately viewed as a modification of which of the following belief systems?

(A) Confucianism
(B) Islam
(C) Christianity
(D) Hinduism

75. Which of the following regions does NOT belong in a list of lands to which Buddhism spread substantially in the centuries following the death of Siddhartha Gautama?

(A) Southeast Asia
(B) Mesopotamia
(C) China
(D) Japan

76. Which is the best estimate for the number of castes that have developed in India over the millennia?

(A) A handful
(B) Dozens
(C) Hundreds
(D) Thousands

77. Which of the following texts contain major religious documents that originated in India?
  I. Vedas
  II. Bhagavad Gita
  III. Koran

(A) I and II
(B) II and III
(C) I, II, and III
(D) I only

78. Which statement comparing classical Chinese civilization with contemporary Western civilization is most accurate?

(A) The Chinese economy relied on slavery to a greater extent than Western civilization did.
(B) China set an enduring pattern of more sophisticated agricultural, metallurgical, and textile production techniques than Western civilization.
(C) Women had markedly greater maneuverability within Chinese civilization to achieve positions of high social status.
(D) The Chinese developed a simplified phonetic writing system similar to Hebrew.

Year	Human Population
3000 BCE	14 million
2000 BCE	27 million
1000 BCE	50 million
500 BCE	100 million

79. Based on the chart above, the rise in population is most directly due to which of the following historical developments?

(A) The rise of early urban centers
(B) An agricultural (Neolithic) revolution
(C) A rise in organized religion
(D) A decrease in job specialization

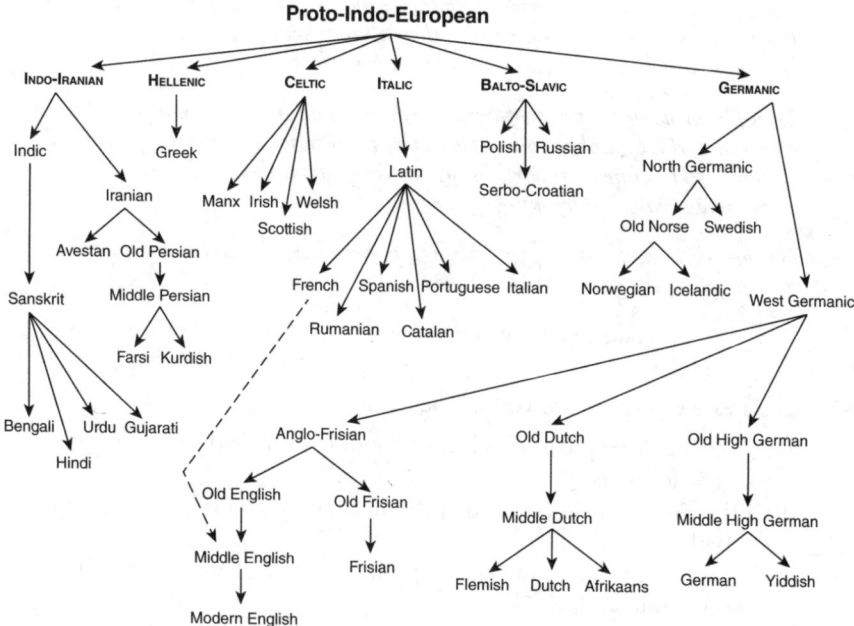

80. The above diagram best demonstrates which of the following historical developments?

(A) Language groups with roots and branches
(B) The migration of hunter-gathering
(C) The rapid spread of writing
(D) Late Roman Empire conquests

81. All of the following languages developed from the Germanic branch of Proto-Indo-European EXCEPT?

   (A) Norwegian
   (B) Icelandic
   (C) English
   (D) Spanish

Hail to thee, O Nile! Who spreads thyself over this land, and comes to give life to Egypt! Mysterious is thy issuing forth from the darkness, on this day whereon it is celebrated! Watering the orchards created by Re, to cause all the cattle to live, you give the earth to drink, inexhaustible one! Path that descends from the sky, loving the bread of Seb and the first-fruits of Nepera, You cause the workshops of Ptah to prosper!

Lord of the fish, during the inundation, no bird alights on the crops. You create the grain, you bring forth the barley, assuring perpetuity to the temples. If you cease your toil and your work, then all that exists is in anguish. If the gods suffer in heaven, then the faces of men waste away.

Then He torments the flocks of Egypt, and great and small are in agony. But all is changed for mankind when He comes; He is endowed with the qualities of Nun. If He shines, the earth is joyous, every stomach is full of rejoicing, every spine is happy, every jaw-bone crushes (its food).

He spreads himself over Egypt, filling the granaries, renewing the marts, watching over the goods of the unhappy.

Source: *Hymn to the Nile* (c. 2100 BCE, author unknown)

82. The above excerpt reinforces that belief in

   (A) The fear Mesopotamians had of flooding of their river valley by incessant rains
   (B) The strongly held beliefs that the ancient Egyptians had for their afterlife
   (C) The reverence for and benefits gained by the Egyptians for their geographic setting
   (D) The dominance of monotheistic beliefs in ancient Egyptian culture

One of the greatest, if not the greatest glory of the Phoenicians was the spread of the alphabet in the Mediterranean area. There is overwhelming consensus among historians and archaeologists that Phoenicians taught the alphabet to the Greeks, and that the Phoenicians and Greeks were responsible for spreading it in the West . . . . This gives the Phoenicians an important role in the history of civilization.

83. Which of the following statements is best supported by this secondary source writing on Phoenician history?

    (A) Phoenicians were "carriers of civilization."
    (B) Phoenicians were the greatest empire builders.
    (C) Phoenicians were ruled by glorious monarchs.
    (D) Phoenicia was a center of philosophy, arts, and sciences.

The disease began, it is said, in Ethiopia beyond Egypt, and then descended into Egypt and Libya and spread over the greatest part of the King's territory. Then it suddenly fell upon the city of Athens, and attacked first the inhabitants of the Peirieus [a port near Athens] . . . . I shall describe its actual course, explaining the symptoms, from the study of which a person should be best able, having knowledge of it beforehand, to recognize it if it should ever break out again. For I had the disease myself and saw others sick of it.

Source: Thucydides, *History of the Peloponnesian War*, 431 BCE

84. Based on the above reading, the disease that spread to ancient Athens was most attributed to

    (A) God's punishment for their polytheistic belief system of multiple deities
    (B) The Greek city's trade and cultural connections around the Mediterranean
    (C) Poor sanitary and unhygienic conditions in Greek cities and countryside
    (D) Invasions from nomadic warriors such as the Huns and Scythians

Source: St. Kevin's church (c. sixth century), Glendalough monastic community in Ireland, 2014. (Photo by Sean McManamon.)

85. The above photo refers to which of the following historical developments?

(A) The spread of Christianity beyond the Roman Empire's borders

(B) The establishment of the papacy in Ireland after Rome fell

(C) The use of Islamic minarets in Irish mosques

(D) The influence of Byzantine law in the British Isles

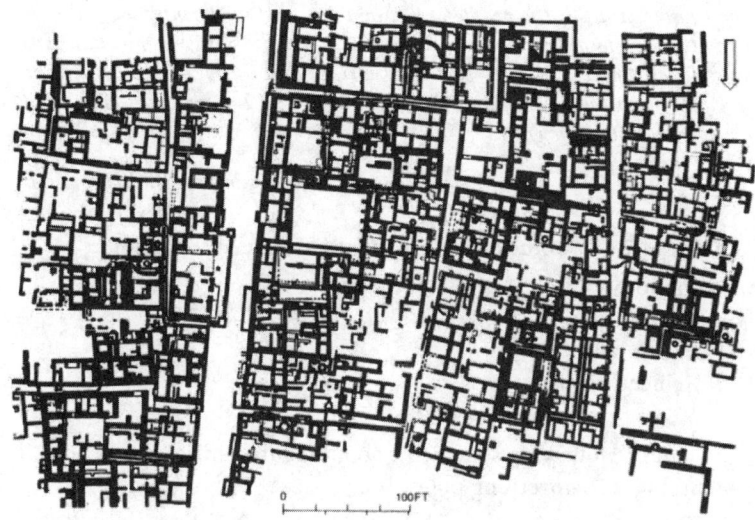

86. The image above shows the ruins of Mohenjo-Daro in modern-day Pakistan, which were part of the remains of the

   (A) Indus River Valley civilization
   (B) Gangetic River Valley civilization in northern India
   (C) Shang civilization along the Yellow River
   (D) Sumerian civilization along the Tigris-Euphrates Rivers

87. The ancient ruins shown above at Mohenjo-Daro in modern-day Pakistan are most famous for achievements in

   (A) Temple ziggurats where they performed ritual sacrifices
   (B) Indoor toilets and sanitation systems built underground
   (C) Floating gardens they used to grow their crops
   (D) A writing system that developed into cuneiform

The Master said, "If the people be led by laws, and uniformity sought to be given them by punishments, they will try to avoid the punishment, but have no sense of shame." "If they be led by virtue, and uniformity sought to be given them by the rules of propriety, they will have the sense of shame, and moreover will become good."

Source: Confucius, *The Analects*

88. Which tenet of Confucianism is expressed in the above passage?

(A) Monotheism
(B) Scholasticism
(C) Filial piety
(D) Reincarnation

89. Which of the following statements about Confucianism shows how revolutionary its governing policy was?

(A) The reciprocal nature of the social system placed responsibilities on the rulers and elites.
(B) The overthrow of the Mandarin scholar official class in traditional China was advocated.
(C) Promoting education of the classics and testing to determine government employment was promoted.
(D) It encouraged peasant societies to rule themselves through peasant agricultural communes.

Stonehenge, England. (Photo by Sean McManamon, 2006.)

90. The photo above of the Stonehenge megaliths in southern England best demonstrates the existence of

(A) Small colonies of Egyptian craftsmen who first settled in southern England

(B) Nomadic groups who were skilled in the building of monumental architecture

(C) Megalithic architecture that was built by scattered groups of hunter-gatherers across Europe

(D) Large populations of settled peoples that were created by the Neolithic Revolution

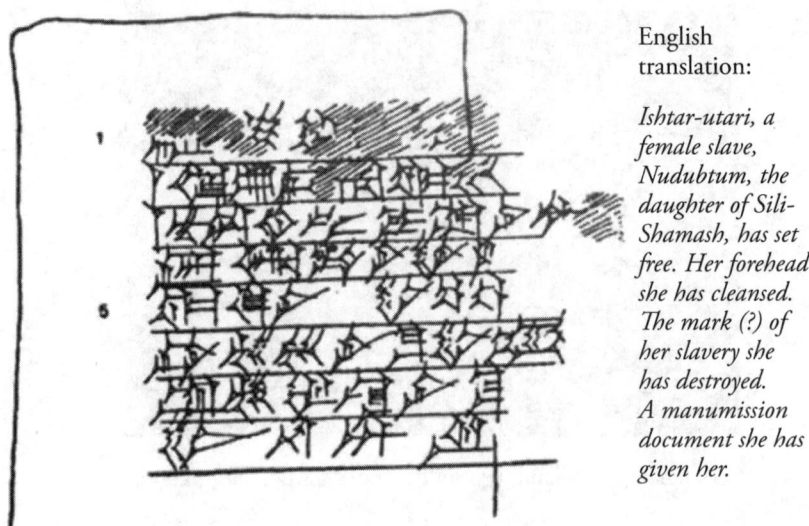

English translation:

Ishtar-utari, a female slave, Nudubtum, the daughter of Sili-Shamash, has set free. Her forehead she has cleansed. The mark (?) of her slavery she has destroyed. A manumission document she has given her.

Source: Babylonian Manumission agreement on a Sumerian clay tablet, c. 2000 BCE

91. Which of the following conclusions is best supported by the image and translation above?

(A) Long-distance slave trade existed between Babylon and ancient Egypt.

(B) Social practices such as the manumission of slaves were recorded.

(C) Economic contracts in Mesopotamia were orally preserved.

(D) Writing was used in Babylon to record the lineage of monarchs.

92. A historian researching the social history of Eurasia in the period 8000 BCE to 600 BCE would most likely find the previous tablet useful as a source of information about which of the following?

(A) The use of religion to encourage manumission of slaves
(B) The spread of writing across the African continent
(C) The diffusion of slavery in the Roman Empire
(D) The use of writing to record social interactions

Name of Chinese Civilization	Dates
Shang	c. 1600–1050 BCE
Zhou	1050–256 BCE
Qin	221 BCE–206 CE
Han	208–220 CE

93. Which Chinese tradition or movement helps explains the information above on traditional China?

(A) Legalism and Daoism
(B) Self-Strengthening Movement
(C) Five Basic Relationships
(D) Mandate of Heaven

94. The fall of the Han dynasty in 220 CE heralded in a period in China of

(A) unprecedented global trade and cultural diffusion
(B) weak regional rulers interspersed with times of disunity
(C) harsh rule by nomadic conquerors from Central Asia
(D) the rebirth of traditional beliefs systems called Neo-Confucianism

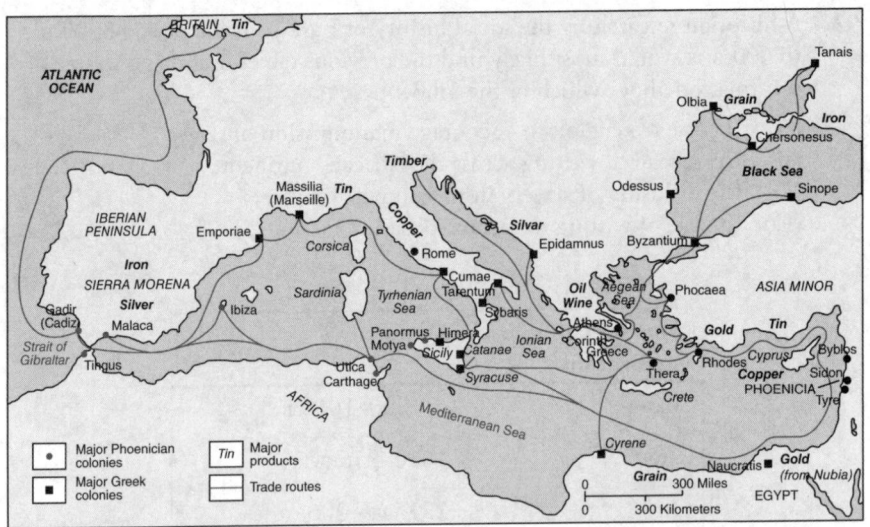

Greek and Phoenician Colonies and Trade. The Western Mediterranean was first colonized by Phoenicians and Greeks who together controlled trade throughout the region.

95. Based on the map above, which of the following conclusions is best supported?

(A) The Greek world consisted of more than the peninsulas and islands of Greece.

(B) Greek colonies were located only in Western Asia and North Africa.

(C) The Greeks were the first settlers in ancient Egypt along the Nile River valley.

(D) Ancient Greek colonies never overlapped with the later Roman Empire.

Roman Coin

96. Based on the image above and your knowledge of history, which of the following conclusions is NOT true?

(A) Metallurgy was adopted from the Etruscans in northern Italy.
(B) The Roman and larger Mediterranean economy was monetized.
(C) Democratic principles and practices were known in ancient Rome.
(D) Writing had not yet been invented or adopted by the Romans.

Blessed are the poor in spirit: for theirs is the kingdom of heaven. Blessed are they that mourn: for they shall be comforted. Blessed are the meek: for they shall inherit the earth. Blessed are they which do hunger and thirst after righteousness: for they shall be filled. Blessed are the merciful: for they shall obtain mercy. Blessed are the pure in heart: for they shall see God. Blessed are the peacemakers: for they shall be called the children of God. Blessed are they which are persecuted for righteousness' sake: for theirs is the kingdom of heaven.

Blessed are ye, when men shall revile you, and persecute you and shall say all manner of evil against you falsely, for my sake. Rejoice, and be exceeding glad: for great is your reward in heaven. . . .

Ye have heard that it hath been said, An eye for an eye, and a tooth for a tooth. But I say unto you, That ye resist not evil: but whosoever shall smite thee on thy right cheek, turn to him the other also.

Source: Holy Bible, King James Version,
Matthew 5:3–13, 5:38–45, 7:7–12

97. Which of the following is best demonstrated by the reading above?

(A) Christianity preached a hatred of non-monotheistic faiths.
(B) Christianity incorporated aspects of social justice.
(C) Christianity beliefs incorporated the Hammurabi Code of Law.
(D) Christianity reinforced a rigid social class structure.

98. The line above "An eye for an eye, and a tooth for a tooth" is a clear reference to the

(A) Babylonian Hammurabi Code of Law
(B) Mesoamerican Aztec Codex
(C) Rome's Twelve Tables of Law
(D) Ancient Egypt's Book of the Dead

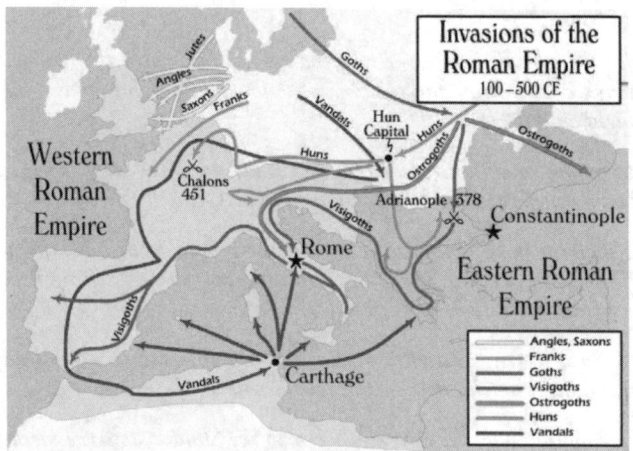

99. One result of the historical development as shown in the above map was the

(A) Decline of Christianity
(B) Growth of the Byzantine Empire
(C) Mongol domination of Europe
(D) Fall of the Western Roman Empire

The Laws of Manu

But for the sake of the prosperity of the worlds, he created the Brahman, the Kshatriya, the Vaishya, and the Shudra to proceed from his mouth, his arms, his thighs, and his feet. . . .

To Brahmans he assigned teaching and studying (the Veda), sacrificing for their own benefit and for others, giving and accepting (of alms).

The Kshatriya he commanded to protect the people, to bestow gifts, to offer sacrifices, to study (the Veda), and to abstain from attaching himself to sensual pleasures. . . .

The Vaishya to tend cattle, to bestow gifts, to offer sacrifices, to study (the Veda), to trade, to lend money, and to cultivate land.

One occupation only the lord prescribed to the Shudra, to serve meekly even these (other) three castes.

The Laws of Manu, c. 200 BCE

100. Based on the reading above, the ramifications of the Laws of Manu on India were

 (A) A funerary ritual
 (B) A polytheistic belief system
 (C) A rigid caste system
 (D) A new pilgrimage route

CHAPTER 2

The Postclassical Era: 600 CE to 1450

Controlling Idea: Resurgence

The story here is rather simple: as we approach the year 600 we see that the classical civilizations have collapsed, and trade and religion lead the way in the process of recovery. The story of this unit is the story of a regeneration of centralized political authority that first matches and then surpasses levels of imperial cohesion seen in the era of classical civilizations. By 1450 a Resurgence has been completed, and broadly speaking each center of civilization has recovered, consolidated, and expanded upon earlier glories. We also notice that by 1450 the major world religions are established, roughly, in the areas they hold sway until today. The great outlier when speaking in such general terms are the civilizations of the Americas which, while developing along familiar lines seen elsewhere in the Foundations era, are not integrated into global networks of long distance trade by 1450.

101. Which of the following would have been outside the sphere of Mongol control at its height?
    (A) China
    (B) Anatolia
    (C) Persia
    (D) Mesopotamia

102. Which long-distance trade network was stabilized in the period historians term the Pax Mongolica (Mongol Peace)?
    (A) Indian Ocean routes
    (B) Triangular trade routes
    (C) East Asian sea routes
    (D) Silk Roads

103. How were individuals selected for leadership in traditional Mongol society?

(A) Hereditary warrior lineage
(B) Long-established aristocratic status
(C) Merit system based on demonstrated battlefield bravery
(D) Divine revelation of chosen ones

104. Which of the following does not belong in a list of military tactics or equipment employed by the Mongol armies?

(A) Combination of light and heavy cavalry
(B) Use of the crossbow and short bow
(C) Phalanx infantry formations
(D) Lightweight armor of leather, iron, or silk

105. Which of the following was the most decisive change Mongol rule brought to Russia?

(A) Emancipation of the serfs
(B) Migration of the center of power from Kiev to Moscow
(C) Permanent separation of Russian culture from that of the West
(D) Abandonment of the Cyrillic alphabet

106. Which of the following dealt the most devastating blow to the Abbasid caliphate in particular and Islamic civilization in general?

(A) Christian crusader incursions in the Near East
(B) Ottoman Turkic conquest of Constantinople
(C) Mongol invasion of Mesopotamia
(D) U.S. invasions of Iraq and Afghanistan after September 11, 2001

107. Which practices were employed by Kublai Khan and later Yuan dynasty rulers to ensure Mongol dominance in China?

  I. Refusal to adopt Chinese civil service exams
 II. Dependence on Muslims and nomads, not Confucian bureaucrats, as next in command in the exercise of power
III. Stubborn clinging to nomadic habits and refusal to settle down and administer the new dynasty from one imperial city

(A) I and II
(B) II and III
(C) I and III
(D) I, II, and III

108. Which group benefited from newfound higher status in the period of Mongol rule in China?

(A) Scholar-gentry
(B) Aristocracy
(C) Peasantry
(D) Merchants

109. Which of the following terms for a political unit does not have the title of its leader as its root word?

(A) Khanate
(B) County
(C) Nation
(D) Shogunate

110. Who led a short-lived reemergence of Central Asian nomadic dominance after the fall of the Mongol Empire?

(A) Suleyman the Magnificent
(B) Kublai Khan
(C) Babur
(D) Timur-I Lang

111. Which military innovation did the Mongols expose Europeans to for the first time?

(A) The catapult
(B) The siege tower
(C) The battle axe
(D) Gunpowder

112. Which global force was the FIRST to consistently integrate sub-Saharan Africa into a global network of exchange of goods and ideas?

(A) Islamic civilization
(B) Modern globalization
(C) Transatlantic slave trade
(D) The Roman Empire

113. Which of the following trade networks is limited to the confines of the African continent?

(A) Triangular trade routes
(B) Indian Ocean
(C) East Asian Sea
(D) Trans-Saharan

114. Which of the following does NOT belong in a list of features of a stateless society?

(A) Delayed ability to respond to external threats
(B) Limited ability to mobilize for war
(C) Mass slave revolt
(D) Difficulty in undertaking large building projects

115. Which of the following was the common unifying feature of sub-Saharan African societies in the postclassical era?

(A) Adoption of Islam by elites
(B) Broad-based expansion of literacy among the masses of the people
(C) Common Bantu linguistic roots
(D) Steam-powered industrial base of the economy

116. As Islam spread, which of the following religious tendencies proved most durable across sub-Saharan Africa?

(A) Ancestor worship
(B) Roman Catholicism
(C) Zen Buddhism
(D) Coptic Christianity

117. North Africa served as a bridge for Muslim influence to reach which region of the globe?

(A) Persia
(B) Central Asia
(C) Anatolia
(D) Spain

118. Since the classical era, which African region most accurately fits the description "gateway to the Middle East"?

(A) Ghana
(B) Zimbabwe
(C) Egypt
(D) Congo

119. Which indigenous African ethnic group adopted and vigorously spread Islam?

(A) Khoisan
(B) Zulu
(C) Berber
(D) Ethiopian

120. Which African society held on most fiercely to Christianity in the period of Islam's expansion in Africa?

(A) Egypt and Ethiopia
(B) Mali
(C) Ghana
(D) Songhai

121. Which does NOT belong in this list of Sudanic states?

(A) Ghana
(B) Mali
(C) Songhai
(D) Congo

122. World historians associate the gold-salt trade most closely with which of the following trade routes?

(A) East Asian sea network
(B) Indian Ocean network
(C) Silk Roads
(D) Trans-Saharan routes

123. Which West African leadership figure is best known for his lavish fourteenth-century pilgrimage to Mecca and Medina?

(A) Kwame Nkrumah
(B) Sundiata Keita
(C) Leopold Senghor
(D) Mansa Kankan Musa

124. Of the postclassical cities listed below, which was the most sophisticated?

(A) Rome
(B) Timbuktu
(C) Paris
(D) London

125. Of the following lists, which places the rise and fall of key West African Sudanic states in proper chronological order?

(A) Mali, Ghana, Songhay
(B) Songhay, Ghana, Mali
(C) Mali, Songhay, Ghana
(D) Ghana, Mali, Songhay

126. Which set of practices carried out by devout Muslims in West Africa set their society apart from patterns established in the greater Islamic world?

(A) Ongoing practice of ancestor worship

(B) Preference of the spoken over the written word in religious and state affairs

(C) Fewer restrictions on female dress codes

(D) Substitution of Timbuktu for Mecca and Medina as a pilgrimage destination

127. Which choice best describes the origins of the Swahili language?

(A) Bantu-Yoruba mix

(B) Arabic-Berber mix

(C) Arabic-Bantu mix

(D) Yoruba-Arabic mix

128. Which choice best describes the points of origin of goods one might find in a Swahili coast market?

(A) Chinese, Indian, English

(B) Islamic, Indian, Chinese

(C) Scandinavian, Indian, Russian

(D) Russian, Islamic, English

129. Which of the following does NOT belong in a list of Swahili states of the East African coastline?

(A) Zanzibar

(B) Mogadishu

(C) Timbuktu

(D) Kilwa

130. Which of the following materials is most associated with premodern sub-Saharan African artistic expertise?

(A) Marble

(B) Oil paints

(C) Mosaic tile

(D) Ivory

131. Which of the following is NOT one of the ways Islam helped strengthen the authority of ruling elites as it spread across the African continent?

(A) Introduction of the written word, which streamlined political administration

(B) Conversion of a majority of commoners, creating a new basis for unity across all classes

(C) Ability to access goods from distant lands through Islamic trade networks

(D) Absorption of techniques of rule from wider Islamic civilization

132. Which of the following does NOT belong in a list of similarities in the process of how Islam spread to South Asia, Southeast Asia, and Africa?

(A) Islam arrived with traders and took root first in urban areas.

(B) The spread of Islam was mainly peaceful.

(C) Political power remained in the hands of non-Arab elites.

(D) A majority of the population in all three areas converted to Islam.

133. Which religious schism stemmed from disputes over legitimate succession of leadership after the death of its key or founding figure?

(A) Eastern Orthodox and Catholic

(B) Catholic and Protestant

(C) Mahayana and Theravada

(D) Sunni and Shia

134. Which best qualifies as the largest durable tricontinental civilization?

(A) Roman

(B) Hellenistic

(C) Islamic

(D) Han

135. Pre-Islamic Arab society is best characterized as

(A) Pastoral nomadic

(B) Sedentary agricultural

(C) Highly urbanized

(D) Maritime trade-based

136. Which two Muslim cities retain the greatest symbolic or religious significance in Islam to this day?
  I. Baghdad
  II. Istanbul
  III. Mecca
  IV. Timbuktu
  V. Medina

  (A) I and II
  (B) II and III
  (C) II and IV
  (D) III and V

137. Which two Muslim cities served as political and administrative centers of Muslim empires?
  I. Baghdad
  II. Istanbul
  III. Mecca
  IV. Mogadishu
  V. Medina

  (A) I and III
  (B) II and IV
  (C) I and II
  (D) III and V

138. Upon whom did Muhammad depend most directly for economic support?

  (A) Local chieftains
  (B) The urban poor
  (C) His wife, Khadija
  (D) Roman imperial administrators

139. Which of the following Arabic terms refers to the "community of the faithful"?

  (A) Hijab
  (B) Hajj
  (C) Hadith
  (D) Umma

140. Which neighboring empires faced the challenge of Umayyad expansion?

    I. Roman
   II. Gupta
 III. Sassanid Persia
 IV. Byzantine
   V. Han

(A) I and II
(B) II and IV
(C) III and V
(D) III and IV

141. Which choice best describes the eastern and western geographic limits of Islamic rule at its greatest extent during the period of the Umayyad and Abbasid caliphates?

(A) Northwest India to Spain and Morocco
(B) Eastern Mediterranean to Persia
(C) Arabian peninsula to the Tigris-Euphrates Valley
(D) Persia to Southeast Asia

142. Who would not have qualified as part of the group labeled the "dhimmi" in the Abbasid caliphate?

(A) Jews
(B) Catholics
(C) Greek Orthodox
(D) Animist

143. Which choice does NOT belong in a list describing the status of Muslim women in the early Islamic period?

(A) Male adultery was condemned in the Koran.
(B) Female infanticide was forbidden.
(C) Females and males both were allowed multiple spouses.
(D) Female inheritance rights were strengthened.

144. In which postclassical civilization did women enjoy the highest status?

(A) Tang China
(B) Islamic
(C) Byzantine
(D) Carolingian

145. Which Muslim group overthrew the Umayyad dynasty and set up a new caliphate?

(A) Sassanids
(B) Seljuks
(C) Abbasids
(D) Swahilis

146. Which city became the capital of the Abbasid Empire and a center of what has been termed an Islamic golden age?

(A) Istanbul
(B) Timbuktu
(C) Seville
(D) Baghdad

147. Which of the following areas of expertise or learning progressed under the rule of the Abbasid caliphate?

(A) Medicine
(B) Law
(C) Philosophy
(D) All of the above

148. Which of the following does NOT belong in a list of characteristics common to the decline of both the Roman and Abbasid empires?

(A) Chaotic succession fights for the imperial throne
(B) Frequent interference of military commanders in politics
(C) Growing dependence on nomadic warriors or mercenaries
(D) Imperial conversion to a new religion

149. What is the name of the peninsula that served as the homeland of the Byzantine and, later, the Ottoman Empire?

(A) Anatolia
(B) Horn of Africa
(C) Iberian
(D) Florida

150. What was the main global impact of the Crusades?
    I. Western Europeans gained permanent bases in the Middle East.
    II. Islam split into the Sunni and Shia branches.
    III. Western Europeans were reintroduced to the knowledge and trade of a more civilized world.
    IV. Christianity became the dominant religion in Jerusalem.

    (A) I, II, and III
    (B) I, II, and IV
    (C) III and IV
    (D) I only

151. The proliferation of technical advances and growing wealth of cities in the Abbasid Middle East was most closely matched by which contemporaneous area of civilization?

    (A) Mississippian North America
    (B) Song China
    (C) Great Zimbabwe
    (D) Western Europe

152. Which region, while under Muslim control, remained the least converted and integrated into the global civilization constructed in the era of the Umayyad and Abbasid caliphates?

    (A) South Asia
    (B) East Asia
    (C) Anatolian Peninsula
    (D) Egypt

153. Which intellectual or technological advancement CANNOT be traced to the era when Islamic civilization was at its height?

    (A) Lateen sails
    (B) Adoption of Arabic numerals
    (C) Anatomical knowledge
    (D) Steam-powered industry

154. Which of the following European regions felt the influence of Byzantine civilization in the postclassical era?

    (A) Russia
    (B) The Balkans
    (C) Ukraine
    (D) All of the above

155. After the fall of the western portion of the Roman Empire, the official tongue in Constantinople shifted from Latin to which of the following?

    (A) Turkish
    (B) Persian
    (C) Chinese
    (D) Greek

156. The Byzantine Empire flourished as a crossroads of trade from which regions?

    (A) Mediterranean, the Middle East, and Asia
    (B) India, Mediterranean, and Asia
    (C) Sub-Saharan Africa, India, and the Middle East
    (D) The Middle East, Asia, and Scandinavia

157. Which early Byzantine emperor had the longest lasting impact on civilization in the eastern Mediterranean and beyond?

    (A) Diocletian
    (B) Constantine
    (C) Justinian
    (D) Osman

158. Which of the following does NOT belong in a list of similarities between Byzantine and dynastic Chinese political rule in the Tang era?

    (A) An imperial bureaucracy staffed by persons from all social classes but generally drawn from the aristocracy
    (B) A throne occasionally held by women
    (C) An emperor whose rule has God's approval
    (D) Focused initiative to expand territorial boundaries of the empire

159. Russian civilization emerged nearest to what modern-day city?

    (A) St. Petersburg
    (B) Kiev
    (C) Moscow
    (D) Warsaw

160. Kievan Rus is unique in world history because

(A) It mediated contact between the Byzantine Empire and more distant lands.

(B) It is the birthplace of Islam.

(C) It was, in land area, the largest single European state of the postclassical era.

(D) It adopted religious and bureaucratic practices from a neighboring civilization.

161. Which ideology gained influence in the period of disorder that followed the collapse of the Han dynasty?

(A) Confucianism

(B) Buddhism

(C) Daoism

(D) Mao Zedong Thought

162. Which dynasty built the largest land empire?

(A) Zhou

(B) Han

(C) Tang

(D) Song

163. Which is most true about the staffing of the central administration of the imperial bureaucracy in the Tang-Song era?

(A) Gifted females were targeted for rapid promotion.

(B) Positions were dominated by sinicized nomads.

(C) Administrators were selected by the emperor.

(D) The staff comprised individuals from prominent families.

164. Which of the following statements best describes the status of the Buddhist faith in China after the persecutions of the Tang era?

(A) Chinese emperors continued to practice Buddhism.

(B) Buddhism grew rapidly as a form of rebellion against a hated imperial bureaucracy.

(C) Buddhism disappeared completely from Chinese society.

(D) Buddhism continued to exist, but on a much reduced scale.

165. Neo-Confucianism incorporated ideas from which of the following belief systems that had grown in popularity in China?

   I. Hinduism
  II. Buddhism
 III. Daoism
 IV. Islam

(A) I and II
(B) II and III
(C) III and IV
(D) I, II, and III

166. Which of the following is NOT a nomadic group that pressured dynastic rule at some point over the course of Chinese history?

(A) Jurchen
(B) Mongol
(C) Turk
(D) Tibetan

167. Which do historians point to as the key infrastructural development of the Tang-Song era?

(A) Construction of the Great Wall
(B) Construction of a national highway system
(C) Construction of the Forbidden City
(D) Construction of the Grand Canal

168. Which practice dates from the Song era?

(A) Foot binding
(B) Arranged marriage
(C) Concubinage
(D) Divorce rights

169. Which is not a native Chinese invention?

(A) Explosive powder
(B) Magnetic compass
(C) Movable type
(D) Steam-powered machinery

170. What is the title earned by students who passed the most difficult battery of Chinese civil service examinations?

(A) Gentry

(B) Ninja

(C) Sensei

(D) Jinshi

171. Which is NOT an effect of the emergence of neo-Confucianism in the Tang-Song era?

(A) Regeneration of a centralized bureaucracy

(B) Preference of Chinese ideas and practices over foreign ones

(C) Growing egalitarianism in gender roles

(D) Development of public works

172. Despite extensive modeling of the Chinese imperial system, how did Japanese civilization hew to established tradition in the postclassical era?

(A) Aristocrats doubled as military officers.

(B) Strict codes of behavior governed noble classes in court life at the imperial center.

(C) Examination systems were not a part of the selection process for the imperial elite.

(D) Poetry was a highly valued art form among the elite.

173. Which of the following peoples would have been outside of the Chinese tribute system in East Asia in the Tang-Song era?

(A) Korean

(B) Vietnamese

(C) Japanese

(D) Polynesian

174. Where in the world did the literary form of the novel emerge?

(A) United States

(B) Japan

(C) France

(D) England

175. Which contemporary society most closely mirrored feudal Japanese patterns of decentralized rule, an economy based on agricultural peasant labor, and emergence of a warrior elite following a distinct code of honor?

(A) Polynesian
(B) Inca
(C) Western European
(D) Russian

176. Which of the following do historians most closely associate with the period of Western history known as the High Middle Ages?

(A) Carolingian France
(B) Steam-powered Industrial Revolution
(C) Enclosure movement and the rise of commercial agriculture
(D) Gothic architecture, the Crusades, and the rise of the Western university

177. Which of the following regions of Western Europe remained most insulated from the general trend toward disorder following the fall of the Roman Empire?

(A) France
(B) England
(C) Germany
(D) Spain

178. Which group was most likely to be literate in the period of European history often called the Dark Ages?

(A) Aristocrats
(B) Peasants
(C) Monks
(D) Knights

The women there have "friends" and "associates" amongst the men out-side their own families, and the men in the same way have "companions" amongst the women of other families. A man may go into his house and find his wife entertaining her "companion" but he takes no objection to it. One day at Iwalatan I went into the qadi's (Islamic judge) house, after asking his permission to enter, and found with him a young woman of remarkable beauty. When I saw her I was shocked and turned to go out, but she laughed at me, instead of being overcome by shame, and the qadi said to me "Why are you going out? She is my companion." I was amazed at their conduct, for he was a theologian and a pilgrim [to Mecca] to boot. I was told that he had asked the sultan's permission to make the pilgrimage that year with his "companion"—whether this one or not I cannot say—but the sultan would not grant it.

Source: Ibn Battuta (a Berber Muslim traveler to Mali), 1351–1353

179. Ibn Battuta's observations indicate the prevalence of which trend in the practice of Islam in postclassical West Africa?

(A) Relaxed attitude towards gender mixing
(B) Strict application of Islamic sharia law
(C) Incorporation of the dhimmi as equals in social status
(D) Organization of society around the principle of jihad

Source: Chichen Itza, Mexico, 2014. (Photo by Sean McManamon.)

180. Based on the above photo of Chichen Itza, which of the following is NOT believed to be true of the ancient Mayans?

(A) They built monumental architecture for religious purposes.
(B) They used these structures for their human sacrifices.
(C) They built these structures as palaces for their emperors.
(D) They used corvee labor as a form of taxation of their subjects.

Spanish colonial-era drawing of Incan with a quipu

181. The image above of the quipu shows that the Incas

(A) Established contacts with ancient Egyptians
(B) Had a fully formed writing system
(C) Wore quipu to ritual human sacrifices
(D) Developed a method of keeping records

In the morning, the emperor sent a message to the patriarch to inform him that a Russian delegation had arrived to examine the Greek faith, and directed him to prepare the church and the clergy, and to array himself in his sacerdotal robes, so that the Russians might behold the glory of the God of the Greeks. When the patriarch received these commands, he bade the clergy assemble, and they performed the customary rites. They burned incense, and the choirs sang hymns. The emperor accompanied the Russians to the church, and placed them in a wide space, calling their attention to the beauty of the edifice, the chanting, and the offices of the archpriest and the ministry of the deacons, while he explained to them the worship of his God. The Russians were astonished, and in their wonder praised the Greek ceremonial. Then the Emperors Basil and Constantine invited the envoys to their presence, and said, "Go hence to your native country," and thus dismissed them with valuable presents and great honor.

Source: *Povest' Vremennykh Let* (*The Russian Primary Chronical*), c. 850–1100 CE

182. The above reading demonstrates which of the following conclusions about Early Russia?

(A) The lay investiture controversy
(B) The Russian invasion of Greece
(C) The polytheistic religion of the ancient Greeks
(D) The Byzantine influence on Russia

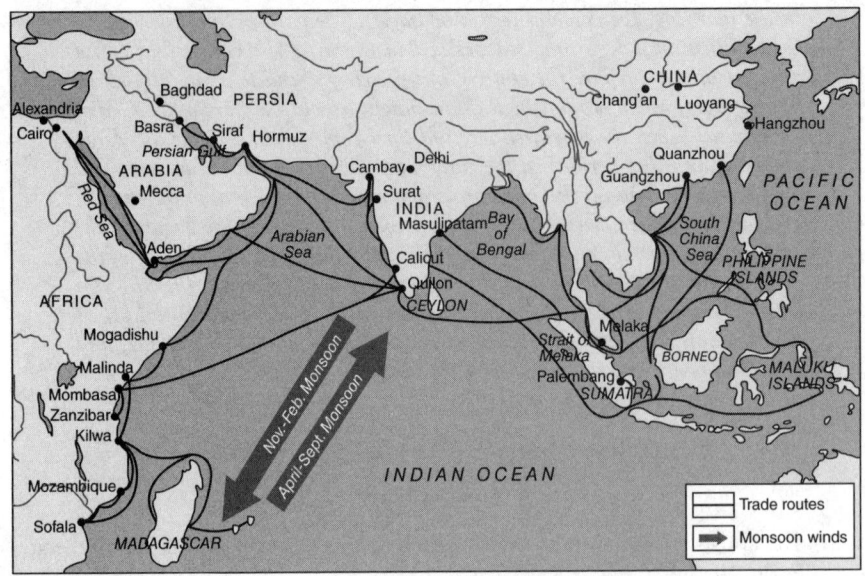

Monsoon Winds

183. The image above shows that trade routes directly linked India in the post-classical era to all of the following regions EXCEPT

(A) China

(B) Middle East

(C) East Africa

(D) Europe

184. The image above question 183 shows that monsoon winds

(A) Facilitated travel from East Africa to South Asia

(B) Brought needed moisture to Central Asia

(C) Contributed to drought and famine in India

(D) Promoted the early use of steamships

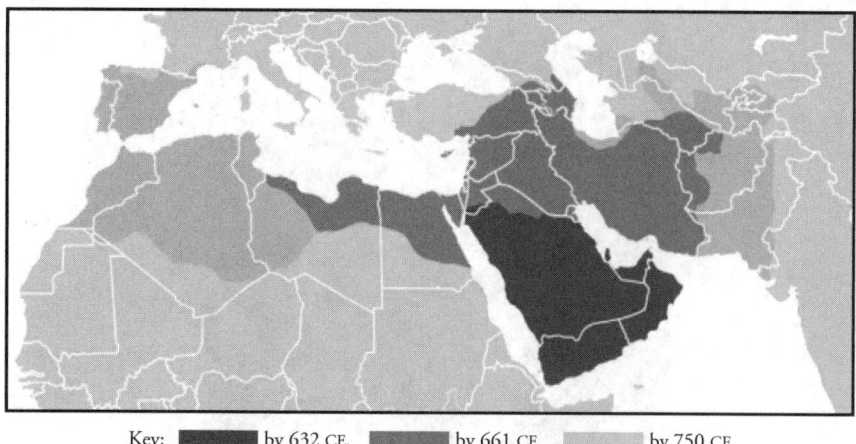

Key: ▮ by 632 CE, ▮ by 661 CE, ▮ by 750 CE

Map of Early Muslim Conquests

185. The Muslim conquests by the eighth century had reached as far west as

(A) Libya
(B) Egypt
(C) The Balkans
(D) Spain

Beware of this world (dunya) with all caution; for it is like to a snake, smooth to the touch, but its venom is deadly. . . . The more it pleases thee, the more thou be wary of it, for the man of this world, whenever he feels secure in any pleasure thereof, the world drives him over into some unpleasantness, and whenever he attains any part of it and squats him down in it, the world turns him upside down. And again beware of this world, for its hopes are lies, its expectations false.

Source: Al-Hasan al-Barri, d. 728 CE

186. The selection above from Islamic tradition was most likely written by which of the following type of individuals?

(A) Palace eunuch
(B) Sufi mystic
(C) Wahhabi imam or cleric
(D) Islamic jurist or judge

Early/Medieval Muslim scientists

187. Based on the image above, which of the following is true of the Abbasid and Umayyad empires?

(A) They taught and tested Confucian values in their schools.
(B) They achieved great advances in the sciences.
(C) They expanded to rule over northern Europe.
(D) They used a Sanskrit form of writing.

Source: Buddhist Temple in Kyoto, Japan. (Photo by Sean McManamon.)

188. The above image proves which of the following statements?

  (A) Indian Hinduism was popular in Japan.
  (B) China exerted a strong influence on Japan.
  (C) Buddhism was rejected by most Japanese.
  (D) Islam was adopted by the Japanese court.

Source: Photo in Vietnam, 2010. (Photo by Sean McManamon.)

189. The above image helps prove which of the following statements?

    (A) Buddhism promotes the monastic lifestyle for its followers.
    (B) Vietnamese men shaved their hair in respect for the Emperor.
    (C) Islamic identity is strong in northern Vietnam.
    (D) Confucian ethics are not promoted in Vietnam.

Special ambassadors [reported] that a monstrous . . . race of men had taken possession of the extensive, rich lands of the east . . . If [the Saracens] themselves could not withstand the attacks of such people, nothing remained to prevent their devastating the countries of the West. . . . [Regarding their] cruelty . . . there can be no infamy [great enough]. . . . The Tartar[s] . . . fed upon their [victim's] carcasses . . . and left nothing but the bones for the vultures.

Source: Matthew Paris, quoted in *Storm from the East*

Their style of conversation is courteous; they . . . have an air of good breeding, and eat their victuals with particular cleanliness. To their parents they show the utmost reverence. . . . The order . . . of all ranks of people, when they present themselves before his majesty ought not to pass unnoticed. When they approach . . . [him] they show their respect . . . by assuming a humble, placid, and quiet demeanor.

—Marco Polo, quoted in *Genghis Khan and Mongol Rule*

190. What impact would Matthew Paris's description have on Europeans?

(A) They would have feared the Mongols as barbaric warriors.

(B) They would have welcomed the Mongols as fellow warrior peoples.

(C) They would have been confused based on the different names Paris used.

(D) They would have been felt confident that Christ would protect them.

191. The above description of the Mongols by Marco Polo

(A) Is a secondary source on the Mongols

(B) Complemented Matthew Paris's account

(C) Reinforced the view of the Mongols as barbaric

(D) Contradicts Matthew Paris's negative account

Angkor Wat

192. The Angkor Wat Temple in Cambodia shows a strong cultural influence from which of the following regions?

(A) Chinese
(B) Persian
(C) Roman
(D) Indian

193. The Angkor Wat Temple was built with influence from which two belief systems?

(A) Hinduism and Buddhism
(B) Islam and Sikhism
(C) Jainism and Hinduism
(D) Confucianism and Daoism

God
there is no god but He, the Living, the Everlasting.
Slumber seizes Him not, neither sleep;
to Him belongs
all that is in the heavens and the earth
Who is there that shall intercede with Him save by His leave?
He knows what lies before them
and what is after them,
and they comprehend not anything of His knowledge
save such as He wills.
His Throne comprises the heavens and earth;
the preserving of them oppresses Him not;
He is the All-high, the All-glorious.

Source: The Quran (also spelled Koran)

194. Which of the following Islamic beliefs is described in the quotation above from the Quran?

(A) Belief in monotheism
(B) Belief in fasting
(C) Belief in the caliphate
(D) Belief in charity

Western Musicians on a Camel, Tang Dynasty

195. Which of the following conclusions can be made?

(A) The diffusion of culture flowed from Japan to China.

(B) Sea links existed with the East African coast.

(C) The use of animal power was replaced by industrialization during the Tang dynasty.

(D) Economic and cultural links existed between Central Asia and the Middle East.

Postclassical Arab/Muslim with astrolabe

196. The image above shows an astrolabe, which demonstrates

    (A) The level of navigational technology of the Abbasids

    (B) The printing available to Islamic lands

    (C) Confucian ritual implements for China

    (D) Portuguese aiming devices for cannons

The mosaic of Emperor Justinian and his retinue

197. The above image shows the Byzantine emperor Justinian flanked by military and ecclesiastical figures. This plus the halo around his head shows that Justinian justified his rule through the principle of

(A) Caesaropapism
(B) Pater familias
(C) Senatorial privilege
(D) Hagia Sophia

Gabriel Ferrand was a French diplomat and an Arabian, Persian, and Malay scholar. In this excerpt from his book *Voyage of Sulayman the Arab Merchant in India and China*, he discusses the business practices of Tang China.

The Chinese conduct commercial transactions and business affairs with equity. When someone lends money to another person, he writes up a note documenting the loan. The borrower writes up another note on which he affixes an imprint of his index finger and middle finger together. Then they put the two notes together, roll them up, and write a formula at the point where one touches the other [so that part of the written formula appears on each note]. Next, they separate the notes and entrust to the lender the one on which the borrower recognizes his debt. If the borrower denies his debt later on, they say to him, "Present the note that the lender gave to you." If the borrower maintains that he has no such note from the lender, and denies that he ever agreed to the note with his fingerprints on it, and if the lender's note has disappeared, they say to him, "Declare in writing that you have not contracted this debt, but if later the lender brings forth proof that you have contracted this debt that you deny, you will receive twenty blows of the cane on the back and you will be ordered to pay a penalty of twenty million copper coins. This sum is equal to about 2,000 dinars [gold coins used in the Abbasid empire]. Twenty blows of the cane brings on death. Thus no one in China dares to make such a declaration for fear of losing at the same time both life and fortune. We have seen no one who has agreed when invited to make such a declaration. The Chinese are thus equitable to each other. No one in China is treated unjustly.

Source: Ferrand, Gabriel, trans., *Voyage du marchand arabe Sulayman en Inde et en Chine*

198. The passage above supports the conclusion of
   (A)   Complex economic practices in Tang China
   (B)   The spread of metal coinage during the Tang dynasty
   (C)   The openness of Tang China to other cultures
   (D)   The taxation of agricultural crops in paper currency

As in West Africa, trade on the continent's east coast brought cultural exchange as well as political changes to the area. As in West Africa, converts to Islam in East Africa tended to first come from the ruling elites. The business connections that literacy in Arabic made possible also stimulated an expansion of reading and writing in this new language. Ruling elites did not give up or replace their religious and cultural traditions though, as established tradition was important for purposes of providing cultural leadership for their societies. Maintaining legitimacy of their rule required adherence to familiar customs. Yet Islam served as a fresh source of legitimacy for their rule as well, since both the political recognition from Islamic states in Southwest Asia, as well as the new wealth and products the elites were able to introduce into their societies were a demonstration of their new-found influence. The conversion of elite classes did not bring about an immediate mass conversion to Islam in East Africa.

199. The secondary source reading above demonstrates which of the following?

   (A) Conversion to Islam in West Africa was from the bottom up.
   (B) West African rulers and elite saw clear benefits in converting to Islam.
   (C) Trade played little role in spreading Islam to West Africa.
   (D) Islam entered Africa from European conquerors.

200. In West Africa, the practice of Islam

   (A) Coexisted with previous forms of worship like animism
   (B) Completely replaced animism and other belief systems
   (C) Linked West Africa directly with Southeast Asia
   (D) Established a caste system similar to that in India

CHAPTER 3

The Early Modern Era: 1450 to 1750

Controlling Idea: The First Global Age

In this unit the big news, so to speak, is that the North and South American continents are integrated into global long distance trade networks for the first time. While all civilizations are in ever closer contact it is the West that works its way to the center of the world trading network, serving as intermediaries in the ever greater volumes of trade that wash across the globe between 1450 and 1750. While not dominant by 1750 (except over the Americas) the West nonetheless is becoming positioned to capitalize off its emergent role at the "core" of a new world economy, and the slow integration of the world into a single economic unit begins in this period and has accelerated down to today.

201. Which of the following does NOT belong in a list of factors preventing European powers from establishing anything more than a limited coastal settlement on the African continent in the period 1450–1750?

(A) Climate
(B) Disease
(C) Impassable rivers
(D) Inferior weapons technology

202. Which European power was first to establish large-scale slave-trading operations on the African continent for the purposes of export to plantations in the Americas?

(A) Spain
(B) England
(C) Portugal
(D) France

203. In which century did the Atlantic slave trade peak in terms of numbers of Africans transported?

(A) Fifteenth
(B) Sixteenth
(C) Seventeenth
(D) Eighteenth

204. Which trend was most typical in slave-capturing coastal West African kingdoms, such as Dahomey, which supplied the Atlantic slave trade?

(A) Mass conversion to Christianity
(B) Increasing hierarchy, centralization, and importance of military capacity including use of firearms
(C) Depopulation as younger generations were shipped away
(D) Industrialization as a result of capital accumulation due to slave trade

205. Which would be the LEAST typical trade transaction along Africa's northeast coast in the period 1450–1750?

(A) Ivory exported to India
(B) Gold exported to Persia
(C) Female slaves exported to Arabian peninsula for domestic labor
(D) Female slaves exported to a West Indies sugar plantation

206. The Afrikaners who settled in southern Africa traced their origin back to which European region?

(A) England
(B) Germany
(C) Netherlands
(D) France

207. What is the best way to characterize relations between the British and the Afrikaners after the British arrived in southern Africa in 1795?

(A) Hostility and complete social segregation
(B) Maintenance of Afrikaner political supremacy
(C) Britain gains formal possession of the colony, but conflict persists with Afrikaners over land and expansion
(D) Complete unity in the face of superior African military strength

208. Which is most true of the Middle Passage?

(A) It was generally a pleasant voyage.

(B) Mortality on marches to the African coast was higher than mortality on the ships.

(C) It generally lasted a year or more.

(D) African naval expertise was key to guiding vessels across the Atlantic.

209. In which New World society did the slave population grow mainly through natural increase and not continued importation?

(A) Haiti

(B) Jamaica

(C) Argentina

(D) Southern British North American colonies

210. Where in the New World did slavery last the longest?

(A) Haiti

(B) Brazil

(C) Cuba

(D) The United States

211. To which location was the greatest number of enslaved Africans transported?

(A) Spanish Mexico

(B) Portuguese Brazil

(C) British North America

(D) Dutch Indonesia

212. Which Western power was first to ban its citizens from engaging in the slave trade?

(A) France

(B) England

(C) United States

(D) Portugal

213. Which Western tradition did the continuation of the Atlantic slave trade violate most?

(A) Enlightenment

(B) Greco-Roman

(C) Feudal

(D) Mercantilist

214. Which monarchy constructed the largest contiguous land empire in history, second in size only to the Mongol Empire?

(A) British
(B) Mughal
(C) Russian
(D) French

215. In which neighboring region(s) did the Russian Empire gain the most land during the Romanov dynasty?

(A) Poland
(B) Baltic States
(C) Black Sea region
(D) Siberia and Central Asia

216. The shift of the Russian imperial capital to which city indicated a shift in orientation toward the West under the rule of Peter the Great?

(A) Moscow
(B) Kiev
(C) Vladivostok
(D) St. Petersburg

217. Which of the following was unique to Russian industrial development in the czarist period?

(A) Use of serf labor in factories
(B) Application of heavy industry to military uses
(C) Growing urbanization
(D) Increased importance of the mining sector of the economy

218. Which of the following best describes the attitude of Peter and Catherine the Great toward adopting change along Western lines?

(A) It was a waste of time and an insult to Russian tradition.
(B) Its harmless influence was allowed to spread without interference.
(C) It was a source of new ideas and methods to increase the power of the ruling family at home and abroad.
(D) It was a key step on the road to Russian democracy.

219. Which Russian territorial possession lay farthest from the center of power in St. Petersburg?

(A) Alaska
(B) Finland
(C) Crimea
(D) Siberia

220. How did Russia tend to fit into the emerging global economy in the period 1450–1750?

(A) As a source of serf labor transported to till the soils of Western Europe
(B) As a market for grain grown in the New World
(C) As the primary Old World destination of the silver being taken out of the New World
(D) As a supplier of grain, timber, fur, and other raw materials to the West

221. Which feature of the expanding Russian Empire in the period 1500–1800 was NOT a feature of expanding Western European empires in this period?

(A) Russia held military dominance over less technologically sophisticated peoples.
(B) Multiple ethnicities fell under the rule of a single monarch.
(C) Territorial expansion was a major goal.
(D) Expansion was mainly carried out over land and not sea.

222. Which end result of industrial development was most important to Peter the Great?

(A) Russian capacity to produce modern weapons
(B) Growth of a vibrant merchant class
(C) A raised cultural level of the resultant urban masses
(D) Ability to project naval power across the Pacific Ocean

223. Which impulse for the colonization of North America was generally missing from the colonization of the rest of the New World?

(A) Setting up slave plantations
(B) The search for gold
(C) Freedom from religious persecution
(D) Expansion of royal authority

224. The economic centrality of long-distance trade and the lack of long feudal traditions opened a path for which social class to rise to dominance relatively quickly in the New World?

(A) Independent farmer/peasant
(B) Proletarian
(C) Merchant
(D) Aristocracy

225. How was racial hierarchy on the North American continent different from racial hierarchy in Spanish Latin America?

(A) Intermarriage among Native American, African, and European populations was much less common.
(B) Enslaved Africans could as a rule look forward to manumission upon the death of his or her owner.
(C) Native Americans were preferred over Africans to perform slave labor.
(D) European settlers formed a smaller minority of the overall population.

226. In which colonized region of the globe did Western cultural practices supplant existing cultural practices most completely after 1450?

(A) West Africa
(B) North and South America
(C) East Asia
(D) South Asia

227. In which way did the Spanish colonies reproduce existing Iberian social structures?

(A) Colonies were established as monarchies in their own right.
(B) Gender roles were preserved from the very start as equal proportions of Spanish males and females settled the New World.
(C) Peninsulares sought to reproduce essentially feudal estates with indigenous labor filling the role of the Spanish serf.
(D) Religious toleration remained an important factor in integrating diverse peoples into a cohesive social unit.

228. Which region of the New World saw the initial penetration by European explorers and subjugation of the Native population to slave labor?

(A) Mesoamerica
(B) Andean South America
(C) Caribbean Islands
(D) Atlantic shoreline of North America

229. Which of the following accompanied the transition from conquest to settlement of the New World?

(A) Transition from the search for gold to setting up of ranches and sugar plantations

(B) Increased emigration of Spanish women to the New World

(C) Disappearance of the majority of the indigenous population through disease or killing

(D) All of the above

230. Which New World commodity was of the greatest value to the Spanish monarchy?

(A) Potato

(B) Tomato

(C) Silver

(D) Sugar

231. What was the long-term impact of the massive influx of silver into the Spanish economy that resulted from its domination of the New World?

I. Inflation and unwise government spending

II. A permanent economic advantage over other European powers

III. Development of the most sophisticated banking system in the world

(A) I only

(B) II only

(C) III only

(D) I and II

232. Which New World commodity was of the greatest value to the Portuguese monarchy in the early phases of the settlement of Brazil?

(A) Potato

(B) Tomato

(C) Silver

(D) Sugar

233. Which of the following choices places Latin America's racial hierarchy in the proper order, from lowest to highest, in status?

(A) Mestizo/mulatto, Native American/African slave, Peninsular, Creole

(B) Native American/African slave, mestizo/mulatto, Creole, Peninsular

(C) Peninsular, Creole, mestizo/mulatto, Native American/African slave

(D) Creole, mestizo/mulatto, Peninsular, Native American/African slave

234. Which statement best characterizes the political situation in the West around 1450?

(A) Highly centralized and powerful monarchies governed linguistically homogeneous kingdoms.

(B) Renaissance ideas had spread, making democracy the preferred political system.

(C) Small political units led by local and regional aristocrats were the rule, not the exception.

(D) The nation-state had taken root and monarchy had passed from the scene.

235. Which label best characterizes the Italian Renaissance?

(A) A political movement

(B) A cultural movement

(C) A religious movement

(D) A mass movement

236. Why did the Renaissance originate in the city-states of northern Italy?

(A) Urban artisans provided financial backing.

(B) Expatriate Chinese artists settled there, provided artistic training.

(C) Urban elites grown rich in trade hubs provided financial backing.

(D) The bubonic plague depopulated the countryside more heavily, destroying rural centers of artistic innovation.

237. Which of the following were targeted in the Spanish "Reconquista" of the late fifteenth century?

(A) Muslims and Huguenots

(B) Huguenots and Jews

(C) Catholics and Jews

(D) Muslims and Jews

238. Which event is most closely associated with the "reintroduction" of the West to the knowledge and trade of the Middle and Far East after the year 1000?

(A) The voyages of Vasco da Gama

(B) The Black Death

(C) The travels of Ibn Battuta

(D) The Crusades

239. Which modern-day European nation projects farthest west off the Eurasian landmass and into the Atlantic Ocean?

(A) Germany
(B) France
(C) England
(D) Portugal

240. Which European naval power is generally credited with breaking the grip on Atlantic maritime trade previously held by the Spanish monarchy?

(A) Holland
(B) Denmark
(C) England
(D) Germany

241. Which of the following does NOT belong in a list of Catholic doctrines rejected by Martin Luther?

(A) Papal authority
(B) Granting of indulgences
(C) Monasticism
(D) Acceptance of the Holy Trinity

242. Where did Luther's movement first take root?

(A) France
(B) England
(C) Spain
(D) Germany

243. Which group traces its roots to the Catholic Reformation, sometimes referred to as the Counter-Reformation?

(A) Benedictine monks
(B) Coptic Christians
(C) Jesuits
(D) Liberation theologians

244. Which social class experienced the most growth in absolute numbers as a result of the commercialization of the Western economy in the period 1450–1750?

(A) Peasantry
(B) Proletarians
(C) Merchants
(D) Aristocracy

245. Which movement from the following list established a tradition of seeking answers to questions about nature through the application of reason and methodical investigation of the world?

(A) Phenomenology
(B) Scientific Revolution
(C) Protestant Reformation
(D) Enlightenment

246. Which of the following movements applied reason to the problems of human affairs and can be understood as an extension of the Scientific Revolution into the field of politics?

(A) Renaissance
(B) Green Revolution
(C) Enlightenment
(D) Protestant Reformation

247. Who is credited with bringing awareness of the heliocentric nature of the solar system into Western civilization?

(A) Aristotle
(B) Galileo
(C) Columbus
(D) Copernicus

248. Which of the following thinkers established the principles of objects in motion and defined the forces of gravity?

(A) Descartes
(B) Rousseau
(C) Newton
(D) Bacon

249. The following ideas from the Declaration of Independence can be attributed most directly to the influence of whom?

We hold these truths to be *self-evident*, that *all men are created equal*, that they are endowed by their *Creator* with certain *unalienable Rights, [71]* that among these are *Life, Liberty and the pursuit of Happiness.* That to secure these rights, Governments are instituted among Men, deriving their just powers from the *consent of the governed,* That whenever any Form of Government becomes destructive of these ends, it is the *Right of the People to alter or to abolish it*, and to institute new Government, laying its foundation on such principles and organizing its powers in such form, as to them shall seem most likely to effect their Safety and Happiness.

(A) John Locke
(B) Rene Descartes
(C) Michel de Montaigne
(D) Alexis de Toqueville

250. Compared, broadly speaking, with other centers of civilization in the world, which of the following had become the most distinctive characteristic of Western intellectual life by about 1750?

(A) Concern with manipulation of nature to serve human interests
(B) Centrality of science in understanding reality
(C) Appreciation of poetry in elite circles
(D) Importance of the written word in preservation of the wisdom of the past

251. Which group suffered the greatest loss of authority as absolute monarchy took hold in the West beginning in the seventeenth century?

(A) Monarchs
(B) Merchants
(C) Peasants
(D) Aristocrats

252. Which of the following kingdoms serves as an exception to the rule of the growing power of absolute monarchies in the West in the period 1450–1750?

(A) Spain
(B) France
(C) Austria-Hungary
(D) England

253. Which event established the basic sovereignty of Parliament over the king of England?

(A) Reform Act of 1832
(B) The Corn Laws
(C) The Magna Carta
(D) The Glorious Revolution

254. The relationship between supply and demand, as well as the concepts of "laissez-faire" and the "invisible hand of the market," can be traced to the writings of

(A) Karl Marx
(B) David Ricardo
(C) Adam Smith
(D) Napoleon Bonaparte

255. Which of the following does NOT belong in a list of principles we can identify with the intellectual movement known as the Enlightenment?

(A) Reason is the way to truth.
(B) Rulers are blessed by the divine.
(C) Humans are naturally good.
(D) Blind faith in religion is wrong.

256. Which of the following is another way to express the immediate precursor to the factory system of production that arose in England that is sometimes termed protoindustrialization?

(A) Specialization of labor
(B) Mass assembly line production
(C) The three-field system
(D) Cottage industry

257. The factories of the Industrial Revolution depended most heavily on the labor of which of the following groups?

(A) Landed peasantry
(B) Aristocracy
(C) Proletarians
(D) Merchants

258. Which of the following branches of Protestantism can trace its roots to a royal figure?

(A) Presbyterian

(B) Calvinism

(C) Lutheranism

(D) Anglican

259. Which of the following effects best captures the impact of the Mongol Empire on world history?

   I. Spread of the bubonic plague across the Eurasian landmass

  II. Stabilization of long-distance trade routes, which sparked greater demand for goods from distant lands

 III. The exposure of old centers of civilization to new religious and intellectual trends

(A) I and II

(B) II and III

(C) I and III

(D) I, II, and III

260. Which statement best characterizes power relations among the centers of Eurasian civilizations as they approached the year 1450?

(A) Islamic caliphates are reaching the height of their power and influence.

(B) Ming rulers of China have redoubled their efforts to move to the center of maritime trading networks in the East Asian and Indian Ocean.

(C) A power vacuum of sorts has opened, as Byzantine, Abbasid, and Ming Chinese powers become less of a force in global affairs.

(D) Western Europe dominates world trade.

261. How do historians explain the Ming dynasty's 1433 decision to abandon the treasure ship voyages to the Indian Ocean basin that could have placed China at the core of the developing world economy?

(A) State resources were required to thwart nomadic incursions from beyond the Great Wall.

(B) A dominant neo-Confucian worldview de-emphasized the value of non-Chinese ideas and products.

(C) State-backed exploration of distant lands was an unusual experiment in Chinese history.

(D) All of the above

262. Which of the following were the first slave-based island plantation colonies set up by Western powers?

(A) Bahamas
(B) Ireland
(C) Canary and Madeiras Islands
(D) Hispanola

263. Which of the following can be characterized as outside the world network of trade in 1450?

(A) Ireland
(B) Scandinavia
(C) East Africa
(D) Mesoamerica

264. We associate the Maori people with which of the following locations?

(A) Tasmania
(B) Azores
(C) New Zealand
(D) Hawaii

265. Which of the following established a line of demarcation separating Spanish and Portuguese claims in the New World?

(A) Treaty of Versailles
(B) Edict of Nantes
(C) Treaty of Westphalia
(D) Treaty of Tordesillas

266. Which European power won the colony of Indonesia away from the Portuguese in the seventeenth century?

(A) England
(B) Spain
(C) France
(D) Holland

267. Which colony was claimed by Spain as a result of Ferdinand Magellan's circumnavigation of the globe in 1519–1521?

(A) Madagascar
(B) Hispanola
(C) Mexico
(D) The Philippines

268. Which event outside the West contributed to creating an opening for the West to move to the core of a global maritime trade network?

(A) Ming reversal of treasure ship voyages in 1433

(B) Fall of the Byzantine Empire after the Ottoman sacking of Constantinople in 1453

(C) Mongol destruction of Abbasid power in 1253

(D) All of the above

269. Which is an example of a new disease Europeans were exposed to as a result of interaction with the peoples of the New World?

(A) Measles

(B) Mumps

(C) Smallpox

(D) Syphilis

270. What was the demographic impact of the Columbian Exchange on the populations of the Old World?

(A) Population growth across the Old World based on New World crops such as corn and the potato

(B) Massive depopulation of Western Europe due to migration to the Americas

(C) Sharp increase in the West African population to furnish individuals for the slave trade

(D) Sharp decrease in male populations as many sailors died at sea

271. In which regional waterways did the West most rapidly emerge into a dominant position after 1450?

(A) Eastern Mediterranean

(B) South China Sea

(C) Arabian Sea

(D) Caribbean Sea

272. What common characteristic can be ascribed to the key cash crops of the period 1450–1750, sugar, tobacco, and coffee?

(A) They require temperate climate to grow.

(B) European indentured servants performed the labor involved in their cultivation.

(C) Revenues from the sale of these goods did not cover the costs of production and transportation.

(D) Each one has addictive qualities.

273. Which of the following regional civilizations was least able to control and regulate its trade relations with the West in the period 1450–1750?

    (A) Safavid Persia
    (B) Tokugawa Japan
    (C) Kongo kingdom
    (D) Ming China

274. Which Western power established trade forts at crucial locations in the Indian Ocean basin including Ormuz, Goa, and Malacca in the early sixteenth century?

    (A) Spain
    (B) England
    (C) Netherlands
    (D) Portugal

275. Which was the first Asian commodity Western merchants were able to gain control over in terms of both production and trade?

    (A) Cotton
    (B) Opium
    (C) Spices
    (D) Porcelain

276. The rule of which Chinese dynasties overlap with the time period 1450–1750?

    I. Yuan
    II. Ming
    III. Qing
    IV. Song

    (A) I and III
    (B) II and IV
    (C) I and IV
    (D) II and III

277. Which three Muslim empires emerged from the wreckage left behind after the Mongol invasions?

    (A) Umayyad, Safavid, Mughal
    (B) Mughal, Safavid, Ottoman
    (C) Abbasid, Ottoman, Umayyad
    (D) Mughal, Umayyad, Abbasid

278. Which is the most distinguishing characteristic of the Safavid civilization when compared to its Ottoman and Mughal empires?

(A) High levels of palace intrigue and violent fights for succession to the throne

(B) Limited public roles for women

(C) Adherence to Shia and not Sunni Islam

(D) Growing interaction with maritime Western powers

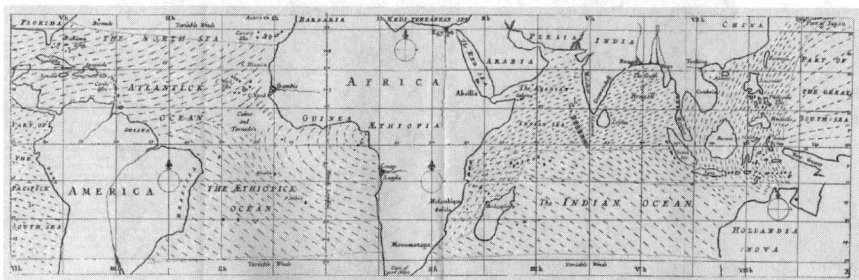

Source: World map showing trade winds by Edmond Halley, 1686

279. The wind currents shown in the map above were used to great effect during which period of long-distance trade and interaction in world history?

(A) The Crusades

(B) The Age of Exploration

(C) The Peopling of Oceania

(D) The Mongol Expansion

280. The trade winds in the Indian Ocean contributed most directly to which of the following?

(A) The spread of Buddhism to the East African coast in the tenth century

(B) The existence of steam technology in navigation during the eighteenth century

(C) The monsoon winds that provided needed water for South Asian agriculture

(D) The use of irrigation canals in ancient Egypt to create surplus crops

Source: "Casta" painting, c. eighteenth century.

281. This work of art which attempts to depict results sexual relations between European, African and Native American (Mestizo, Indian and "coyote") is best understood in the context of which historical process?

(A) The Spanish and Portuguese conquest of the Americas

(B) The capture of slaves in the interior of the African continent

(C) The nineteenth-century Latin American independence movements

(D) The Reconquista in the Iberian Peninsula by Christian forces

282. The image above question 281 best demonstrates which of the following conclusions about Colonial Latin America in the 1500s to 1800s?

(A) Strong industrial base and infrastructure
(B) A predominantly Christian populace
(C) A decline in agriculture and trade
(D) Sharp racial and class divisions

> 1. *Japanese ships are strictly forbidden to leave for foreign countries.*
>
> 2. *No Japanese is permitted to go abroad. If there is anyone who attempts to do so secretly, he must be executed. The ship so involved must be impounded and its owner arrested and the matter must be reported to the higher authority.*
>
> 3. *If any Japanese returns from overseas after residing there, he must be put to death.*
>
> 4. *If there is any place where the teachings of padres (Christianity) is practiced, the two of you must order a thorough investigation . . .*
>
> 7. *If there are any Southern Barbarians (Westerners) who propagate the teachings of padres, or otherwise commit crimes, they may be incarcerated in the prison maintained by the Omura domain, as previously . . .*
>
> 10. *Samurai are not permitted to purchase any goods originating from foreign ships directly from Chinese merchants in Nagasaki.*
>
> Source: *The Edicts of the Tokugawa Shogunate,* 1615

283. Which of the following conclusions about the period from the seventeenth to the nineteenth century is most directly supported by the passage above?

(A) Japan was unified late in history, necessitating a need for a strong central government.
(B) Being a peninsular nation, Japan saw itself as a separate identity from Asia.
(C) Japan's adoption of Buddhist beliefs brought with it a distrust of merchant activity.
(D) Japan's elites feared by that a spread of Western influence would undermine their rule.

284. Compared to the regulations in the excerpt, Ming Chinese policies concerning interactions in the early modern era differed in that they

(A) Initially saw the Christian missionaries and European traders as just another group that wanted tributary status with the Chinese empire

(B) Sought to ban all interaction with outside peoples after Mongol domination in the twelfth and thirteenth centuries

(C) Opened its doors to all foreign interaction after years of isolation and falling behind technologically

(D) Promoted the spreading of Japanese culture to mutually benefit Asian peoples against the threat of European domination

Empire	Land Area	Approximate Population	Religious Composition	Estimated Size of Military	Source of Canons/ Firearms
Ottoman Empire c. 1566	c. 1,200,000 square miles	20–35 million	Large majority Sunni; a significant Christian and small Jewish minorities	Largest army Recorded: 200,000 cavalry, infantry, artillery +90 warships	Produced locally
Safavid Empire c. 1600	c. 750,000 square miles	10–15 million	Majority Shi'a Muslim; small Sunni, Jewish, and Christian minorities	40,000-50,000 cavalry, infantry, artillery; no navy	Imported cannon not widely used, except by European mercenaries
Mughal Empire c. 1600	c. 1 million square miles	105–110 million	Ruling Muslim minority with great Hindu majority plus Sikh, Buddhist, Jain, and Christian minorities	200,000+ cavalry, infantry, artillery; no navy	Imported and produced locally

285. Which of the following conclusions is best supported by the data in the chart above?

(A) The spread of gunpowder weaponry helped these states dominate and retain power.

(B) The importation of gunpowder weaponry limited the reach of these states to Asia.

(C) Gunpowder eliminated forever the use of cavalry on Eurasian battlefields.

(D) The spread of gunpowder weaponry was initiated by Christian and Jewish minorities.

286. Based on a study of the chart above question 285, a historian of Muslim rule in the Early Modern World (1450–1750) would most likely support which of the following historical arguments?

(A) The military might of Jewish minorities in the Middle East was a challenge for the Ottomans.

(B) The Safavid empire easily dominated its Muslim neighbors, the Ottomans and Mughals.

(C) Mughal rulers had a more difficult task of ruling over a large non-Muslim population.

(D) With no Mughal navy, Mughals traders did little business with the outside world.

287. All of the following best explains the existence of a large Hindu majority in South Asia by the Mughal era EXCEPT

(A) Islam's relatively late arrival in a South Asia

(B) Hinduism's long establishment and state support

(C) Islam offered social equality among its followers

(D) Hinduism absorbed many Buddhist and Jain beliefs

Source: Photos from the Hagia Sophia in Istanbul, Turkey, showing minarets and large decorative shields with calligraphy inscriptions from the Koran. (Photos by Sean McManamon.)

288. The addition of Islamic minarets and the shields to the Hagia Sophia church after the Ottoman conquest of the Byzantine Empire and its capital city Constantinople is a result of all of the following EXCEPT

(A) Appropriation by a triumphalist Islam over Christianity
(B) Conquest of Constantinople by the Ottoman Turks
(C) Cultural blending of Islamic and Christian design
(D) The welcoming of Muslims to the Byzantine church

Our Confucian teaching is based on the Five Relationships (between parent and child, ruler and [subject], husband and wife, older and younger brothers, and [between] friends), whilst the Lord of Heaven Jesus was crucified because he plotted against his own country, showing that he did not recognize the relationship between ruler and subject. Mary, the mother of Jesus, had a husband named Joseph, but she said Jesus was not conceived by him.

Those who follow this teaching [Christianity] are not allowed to worship their ancestors and ancestral tablets. They do not recognize the relationship of parent and child. Their teachers oppose the Buddhists and Daoists, who do recognize the relationship between ruler and subject and father and son. Jesus did not recognize the relationship between ruler and subject and parent and child, and yet the Christians speak of him as recognizing these relationships. What [arrogant] nonsense! . . .

Source: Yang Guangxian, c.1659–1665

289. The attitudes in the passage above are best understood in the context of which of the following?

(A) Pro-Buddhist and Daoist sentiments
(B) Anti-Christian and xenophobic attitudes
(C) Chinese tribute and trade systems
(D) Chinese abandonment of Confucianism

290. The attitudes in the passage above question 289 were most commonly expressed by which of the following people in Chinese society?

(A) Taoists hermits
(B) Muslim traders
(C) Confucian scholars
(D) Buddhist monks

Print showing the French King, Louis XIV, visiting the Academy of the Sciences in 1671

291. Based on the image above, which of the following was a cause of the Scientific Revolution in Europe during the seventeenth and eighteenth centuries?

(A) Royal patronage and support
(B) The trial of Galileo Galilei
(C) The palace of Versailles
(D) The spread of gunpowder

292. Compared to the result depicted in the image above question 291, a Scientific Revolution did not come to Asia because of which of the following?

(A) Asia was completely isolated from West and refrained from trade and contact.

(B) Asia had little experience with literacy and lacked an educated scholar class.

(C) Asian monarchs were primarily interested in conquest and less in art and science.

(D) Intellectual curiosity was being stifled by a strict adherence to belief systems.

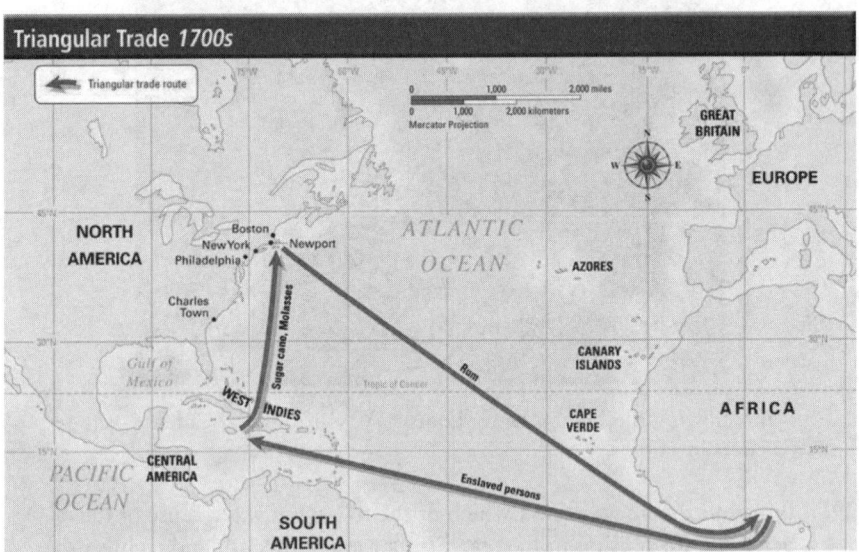

293. A historian would most likely use the map above in studying which of the following?

(A) Immigration patterns around the world

(B) Triangular trade network across the Atlantic

(C) Industrialization across the Americas

(D) The market for luxury goods in Africa

294. Which economic system was in place when the exchange of goods shown in the map above question 293 arose?

(A) European mercantilist laws
(B) Laissez-faire principles
(C) Renaissance guild by-laws
(D) Medieval manorialism

Luther Before the Diet of Worms, 1521, by Anton von Werner

295. The image depicts Martin Luther answering to Holy Roman Emperor Charles V. Which relationship between church and state best describes Catholic Western Europe in the early modern era?

(A) Rulers created new religions to unify conquered peoples.
(B) Rulers asserted that royal laws were superior to divine laws.
(C) Rulers deferred to secular authorities in regulating heresy.
(D) Rulers had a symbiotic close relationship with religious authorities.

296. Martin Luther's popularity and survival was due in large part to which of the following factors?

(A) Printing press technology
(B) Black Death/bubonic plague
(C) Gold imports from the Americas
(D) Roman Catholic reforms

Traditional rice agriculture in Vietnam, 2010. (Photo by Sean McManamon.)

297. The photo above shows the rice agriculture in the Mekong River delta. Which of the following statements is NOT true?

(A) Rice agriculture is heavily dependent on seasonal rains.
(B) Like potatoes, rice requires little farm labor and care.
(C) Rice is an Old World crop common in Asia.
(D) Various strains of rice are grown throughout Asia.

Today's students in large numbers skip over [texts]. From their youth they have already practiced writing essays, and do not know how to progress gradually in the proper sequence. In teaching children of seven and eight years of age, please let them be taught to read the Classics of Loyalty and Filial Piety first, as well as the Four Books which belong to primary studies. Only afterwards let lecturing on the Five Classics and philosophy and history be continued.

Source: The Nguyễn Court's Comments on Scholarship and the Examinations, 1737

298. The above passage from Vietnam demonstrates

(A) The strong Chinese influence in Vietnam
(B) The government rejection of Confucian values
(C) The spread of literacy from Europe
(D) The close connection to India

What kind of man is this Buddha who makes a son that should carry on the family line betray his father and sever the affection between father and son; who makes men resist the Son of Heaven and destroy the righteousness between lord and minister; who says that for men and women to live together is not the Way; who says that for men to plow and women to weave is not righteous, thus severing the way of generating life and blocking off the source of food and clothing; and who thinks that through his way he can transform all under heaven?

Source: Excerpt from the *Koryŏ sa: Pak Ch'o, Anti-Buddhist Memorial*,
c. 1400 CE

299. Based on the reading above, what aspect of Buddhism is the author attacking?

(A) The promotion of a monastic lifestyle
(B) Its Chinese and therefore foreign origins
(C) An embargo of Korea food and clothing
(D) Its promotion of literacy for women

 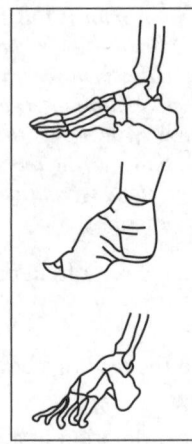

Chinese girl with bound feet

300. Which of the following conclusions is best supported by the two images above?

(A) Chinese society supported female empowerment.
(B) Chinese society was heavily influenced by Vietnam.
(C) Chinese society was a strict patriarchy.
(D) Chinese society practiced Social Darwinism.

CHAPTER 4

The Modern Era: 1750 to 1914

Controlling Idea: The Rise of Capitalism

Capitalism, put simply, is an economic and social system where the needs of capital come first. Capital is wealth that is invested to generate more wealth. In 1750 capitalism was in its infancy and did not shape life in a significant way outside the West and its New World colonies. By 1914 there was not a corner of the globe that had not been impacted by the growth of this dynamic new economic force. The political corollary of these economic changes was that the old feudal and monarchical systems of rule were overthrown and undermined in a series of events that took off on a global scale in the wake of the French Revolution. The key turning point in driving such far reaching change was an Industrial Revolution made possible in the new economic, technological, and political climate fostered by the Rise of Capitalism.

301. Which of the following was a new Western motive for overseas territorial expansion in the industrial era?

    (A) Missionary drive to convert non-Western peoples to Christianity
    (B) Seizure of land to be put to use raising cash crops
    (C) Drive to dominate sources of precious minerals and metals
    (D) Need for raw materials for factory production

302. How did the Dutch gain control of Java?

    (A) Massive emigration from the Netherlands to Indonesia gave the Dutch a demographic advantage.
    (B) Rapid industrialization and urbanization allowed for management of the majority of the population at work and at home.
    (C) Shrewd exploitation of existing political divisions on the island resulted in territorial concessions.
    (D) Supremacy in military technology resulted in direct rule after an initial period of warfare.

303. Which rival European power did the British defeat in the eighteenth century in its drive to control the Indian subcontinent?

(A) Netherlands
(B) France
(C) Italy
(D) Portugal

304. Which of the following was NOT a reason India had become Britain's most important colony by about 1800?

(A) India offered crucial port facilities for the British navy.
(B) India was a major outlet for British manufactured goods.
(C) India was an important supplier of British raw materials.
(D) India was an important location for British textile factories.

305. During the era of British colonialism in India, why were the British content, in general, to leave Indian social hierarchies intact?

(A) Over time, exposure to Hindu doctrine on caste won British elites over.
(B) British officials were able to, in essence, graft themselves onto an existing social pyramid at its apex while incurring a minimum of social disruption.
(C) British notions of proper gender roles, such as a wife's duty to commit sati were the same as Indian ones.
(D) Superior Mughal political and military authority prevented British interference in Indian social relations.

306. In which area did British and Dutch colonialists in South Asia and Indonesia assimilate the fewest indigenous practices?

(A) Religion
(B) Dress
(C) Food
(D) Housing

307. By what method did Western imperialists work to gain a dependable corps of local managers to aid in the administration of their colonies?
   I. Kidnapping of managers' family members and holding them for ransom
   II. Conversion of local elites to Christianity
   III. Education of new generations of colonized youth in Western languages and cultural practices
   (A) I and II
   (B) II and III
   (C) I and III
   (D) II only

308. Which event highlighted widespread corruption and mismanagement among British East India Company administrators?
   (A) Robert Clive's victory at the Battle of Plassey in 1757
   (B) Chaotic departure of British forces in 1947
   (C) Decision to fire on unarmed crowds at Amritsar in 1918
   (D) Famine in Bengal in the 1770s

309. Which reform was most emblematic of growing British interest in transforming Indian social relations in the nineteenth century?
   (A) Dismantling of the caste system
   (B) Prohibition of sati
   (C) Expansion of education for girls
   (D) Building interest in the sport of cricket

310. Which answer choice contains the major rivals to British industrial and imperial supremacy that emerged in the second half of the nineteenth century?
   (A) China, Belgium, Germany, the United States
   (B) The United States, Brazil, France, Germany
   (C) China, Brazil, Germany, Belgium
   (D) The United States, Belgium, France, Germany

311. Which of the following factors best describes international relations among the Western powers in the decades leading up to 1914?

   I. Rivalry involving colonial spoils, arms races, and alliance formation
   II. Major direct military clashes in colonial portions of the globe
  III. Mutual disinterest in territorial and military advances

(A) I and II
(B) II and III
(C) I and III
(D) I only

312. Which answer choice contains regions that were nominally independent but nonetheless endured significant Western informal political and economic influence by 1914?

(A) West Africa, South Asia, China, Latin America
(B) China, Persia, the Middle East, Latin America
(C) Persia, West Africa, South Asia, Latin America
(D) South Asia, the Middle East, China, Latin America

313. Which of the following does NOT belong in a list of contested settler societies?

(A) Algeria
(B) India
(C) South Africa
(D) Kenya

314. Which of the following is generally true of indigenous individuals promoted to assist Western imperialists in their rule of the colony?

(A) When possible, Christians were chosen.
(B) They tended to be from minority ethnic groups.
(C) They were given limited Western education and technical training.
(D) All of the above

315. Which of the following best characterizes the difference between educational systems set up by imperialists in Africa and India?

(A) African colonies contained comparatively more schools administered by colonial governments than India.
(B) African schools tended to be set up by Christian missionaries while Indian ones were set up by the colonial state.
(C) Indian education mainly consisted of trade schools for training industrial workers, while African schools did not.
(D) African education mainly consisted of trade schools for training industrial workers, while Indian schools did not.

316. Which sector of the colonized economy had experienced the least expansion by 1914?

(A) Transport
(B) Mining
(C) Export crop cultivation
(D) Heavy industrial capacity

317. The purpose of the Berlin Conference of 1885 was

(A) For representatives of Western industry to learn cutting-edge German industrial techniques
(B) For representatives of colonized peoples to learn cutting-edge German industrial techniques
(C) To set quotas and agreements surrounding the growth of the German navy
(D) To negotiate settlements among Western rivalries over the partition of Africa

318. The India Congress Party's early membership consisted heavily of middle-class individuals, including M. K. Gandhi, trained in which profession?

(A) Journalism
(B) Engineering
(C) Law
(D) Policing

319. Which choice lays out the correct order in which the Industrial Revolution began and spread?

(A) Great Britain, United States, continental Europe
(B) Continental Europe, United States, Great Britain,
(C) United States, continental Europe, Great Britain
(D) Great Britain, continental Europe, United States

320. Which of the following ran counter to the democratic impulses associated with the American Revolution?

(A) Rejection of aristocratic notions of hierarchy in the thirteen colonies
(B) Continued centrality of slavery to the colonial socioeconomic order
(C) New England's tradition of town meetings
(D) Virginia's practice of election of a House of Burgesses

321. Which list places key events of the French Revolution in proper chronological order?

(A) Formation of National Assembly, Reign of Terror, Directory, rule of Napoleon

(B) Reign of Terror, rule of Napoleon, formation of National Assembly, Directory

(C) Directory, rule of Napoleon, formation of National Assembly, Reign of Terror

(D) Formation of National Assembly, Reign of Terror, rule of Napoleon, Directory

322. Which of the following documents spells out Enlightenment ideas as they were applied to revolutionary France?

(A) The Declaration of Independence

(B) *Second Treatise of Government*

(C) *The Social Contract*

(D) *Declaration of the Rights of Man and Citizen*

323. Which group emerged at the peak of French social status as a result of the French Revolution?

(A) Urban proletariat and artisans

(B) Aristocracy

(C) Clergy

(D) Bourgeoisie

324. Which statement best characterizes the response of ruling elites in neighboring Western powers to the toppling of the French monarchy?

  I. Indifference
 II. Military intervention
III. Imitation

(A) I only

(B) II only

(C) III only

(D) I and II

325. Historians estimate the numbers of victims in the Reign of Terror in roughly what figures?

(A) Hundreds

(B) Thousands

(C) Tens of thousands

(D) Hundreds of thousands

326. Which traditions of the French Revolution did not survive long beyond the initial and radical phases?

(A) Equality under the law
(B) Attack on feudal privilege and institutions
(C) Popular nationalism
(D) Women's leading role in toppling established political powers

327. Which nineteenth-century political ideology stressed principles of laissez-faire and constitutional rule?

(A) Conservative
(B) Liberal
(C) Fascist
(D) Anarchist

328. Which answer choice includes the major political groupings in nineteenth-century Europe?

(A) Conservative, liberal, radical
(B) Liberal, radical, fascist
(C) Fascist, conservative, radical
(D) Radical, fascist, anarchist

329. Which of the following Western societies escaped internal disturbances during the Revolutions of 1848?

(A) Germany
(B) Austria
(C) Hungary
(D) Russia

330. Which of the Western societies expanded democratic rights in the first half of the nineteenth century but did not experience the mass upheavals of 1848?

I. Great Britain
II. France
III. The United States

(A) I and II
(B) II and III
(C) I and III
(D) I, II, and III

331. Which of the following was NOT an influential political force in Europe by the late nineteenth century?

(A) Feminism
(B) Social democracy
(C) Socialism
(D) Absolute monarchy

332. Which of the following does NOT belong in a list of new responsibilities Western governments gained in the nineteenth century?

(A) Public education
(B) Workplace safety regulation
(C) Child labor regulation
(D) Minimum-wage regulation

333. Who does NOT belong in a list of nineteenth- and early twentieth-century rationalist thinkers?

(A) Karl Marx
(B) Albert Einstein
(C) Sigmund Freud
(D) John Locke

334. Among Western settler societies, which had emerged as the leading industrial power by 1914?

(A) Canada
(B) New Zealand
(C) Australia
(D) The United States

335. Which of the following did most to set the United States apart as unique within Western civilizations in the nineteenth century?

(A) Persistence of racialized slavery
(B) Levels of urbanization
(C) Industrial development
(D) Territorial size

336. The rise of which industrial power in the decades leading to 1914 upset the established diplomatic and economic order among Western powers that had existed throughout much of the nineteenth century?

(A) France
(B) Great Britain
(C) Germany
(D) Sweden

337. Which answer choice best captures the changes historians associate with what is termed the "second industrial revolution"?

(A) Industrialization outside of England
(B) Shift to nuclear power in the West after World War II
(C) Central role of heavy industry and electrical power
(D) Rapid urbanization associated with factory production

338. Upon which demand would radicals and liberals have most likely agreed?

(A) Worker control of industry
(B) Minimum-wage laws
(C) Expansion of voting rights
(D) A graduated income tax

339. Which of the following causes did the American and French Revolutions share?

I. Frustration over high levels of taxation
II. Resentment at exclusion from governmental decision making
III. Anger sparked by feudal exploitation of the peasantry

(A) I and II
(B) II and III
(C) I and III
(D) I only

340. Which of the following is a consequence and not a precondition of industrial development?

(A) Capital accumulation
(B) Abundant labor supply
(C) Organized labor union movement
(D) Technical know-how

341. Which thinker is most closely associated with formulating the theories of "Social Darwinism"?

(A) Karl Marx
(B) Jean-Jacques Rousseau
(C) Thomas Hobbes
(D) Herbert Spencer

342. Which group of formerly colonized nations gained political independence from Western colonialism in the nineteenth century?

(A) Ghana, Mexico, India
(B) Argentina, Mexico, Brazil
(C) India, Mexico, Brazil
(D) Brazil, India, Ghana

343. Which situation did formally independent Latin American nations have most in common with colonized portions of Africa and Asia in the nineteenth century?

(A) Rapidly expanding social, economic, and political possibilities for the majority of women
(B) A dependent position in the world economy due to the rise of Western industrial capitalism
(C) Declining importance of race and ethnicity in defining social status
(D) Supplantation of agriculture by industry as the main occupation of the laboring population

344. Which of the following concerns made Creole elites, who yearned for independence from Spain, what we might call "cautious revolutionaries"?

(A) Fear that the Spanish monarchs were more capable rulers
(B) Fear that continued rapid industrialization would create urban instability
(C) A growing communist threat inspired by the example of the Bolshevik Revolution in the Soviet Union
(D) Fear that slaves and other oppressed groups would target local elites as part of a general social upheaval

345. After the United States, which was the next New World colony to gain independence from European power?

(A) Mexico
(B) Argentina
(C) Brazil
(D) Haiti

346. Which event in Europe contributed most directly to the wave of independence struggle in early nineteenth-century Latin America?

(A) Publication of the Gutenberg bible
(B) The Reconquista
(C) Napoleon's invasion of Spain
(D) Fascist aerial bombardment of Guernica

347. Why was the struggle for Brazilian independence distinctive in Latin American history?

(A) Brazil was the only colony whose economy was dependent on cash crops.

(B) Brazil remained a monarchy after independence.

(C) Brazil abolished slavery before independence was achieved.

(D) Brazil was the first colony to achieve independence.

348. Which social practices of the early United States were replicated in newly independent Spanish Latin America?

(A) Slavery was maintained.

(B) Women remained subordinate to men.

(C) Property restrictions were placed on voting.

(D) All of the above

349. Which is the best reason why rail networks were underdeveloped in Spanish Latin America at the time independence was achieved?

(A) Colonial-era Latin American mining was not profitable enough to warrant rail investment.

(B) No cash crops were produced for export.

(C) Rail technology was relatively new and limited to small areas of Britain, Western Europe, and the United States at the time.

(D) Latin American mountains and rivers made rail construction impossible.

350. What impact did the instability of the wars for independence have on subsequent developments in Latin America?

(A) Agricultural regions devastated by modern warfare were slow to recover, leading to widespread famine.

(B) Female veterans of military service refused subordinate roles in the home.

(C) Military leaders remained influential and intervened frequently in political affairs.

(D) Mestizo, slave, and indigenous populations formed guerrilla units and launched armed struggle for communism.

351. Which set of opposing political groupings would be most likely to disagree chiefly over the power of local versus national government?

(A) Fascist and Communist

(B) Democrat and Republican

(C) Anarchist and Liberal

(D) Centralist and Federalist

352. What was the main commonality Liberal and Conservative politicians shared in nineteenth-century Latin America?

(A) They agreed that the Catholic church had too much power.
(B) Both were led by wealthy landowners and the urban middle to upper classes.
(C) They agreed on the immediate abolition of slavery and repatriation to Africa.
(D) Both looked with admiration on the example of independent Haiti.

353. What best characterizes relations between newly independent Latin American nations and British power in the mid-nineteenth century?

(A) Mutual indifference
(B) British indifference to Latin American requests for alliance
(C) British naval assistance in defense of Latin American independence in exchange for access to Latin American consumer markets and raw materials
(D) Latin American trade protectionism in the face of British exports to stimulate local industrial development

354. Which area of the Latin American economy was most damaged by free-trade relations with the British?

(A) Rail
(B) Port city
(C) Manufacturing
(D) Ranching

355. Which does NOT belong in a list of the most important Latin American exports to the industrial West in the second half of the nineteenth century?

(A) Beef
(B) Coffee
(C) Grains
(D) Gold

356. War with which Western power reduced Mexico's territory by about half?

(A) The United States
(B) France
(C) Spain
(D) Portugal

357. Which choice best characterizes the top priorities of the liberal regime of Mexican leader Benito Juarez?

   (A) Constitutional rule with reduced privileges for church and military elites
   (B) Land reform to satisfy the needs of an impoverished peasantry
   (C) Maintenance of privileges for church and military elites
   (D) Rapid industrialization by way of a planned economic system

358. Which independent Latin American nation saw the defeat of the last unassimilated indigenous group willing to take up armed struggle to defend its autonomy?

   (A) Argentina
   (B) Mexico
   (C) Cuba
   (D) Venezuela

359. Which Latin American nation attracted the greatest number of European immigrants in the late nineteenth and early twentieth centuries?

   (A) Colombia
   (B) Peru
   (C) Venezuela
   (D) Argentina

360. Which best characterizes the rule and impact of Porfirio Diaz in Mexico?

   (A) Sacrifice of liberal political principles in pursuit of industrial and infrastructural modernization
   (B) Peasant-based populist mandate achieving comprehensive land reform
   (C) Puppet ruler manipulated by German imperialism bringing little to no economic development
   (D) Conservative ruler who returned large landowners and Catholic elites to power

361. Where did U.S. influence expand most greatly as a result of the Spanish-American War?

   (A) Mexico
   (B) Cuba
   (C) Puerto Rico
   (D) B and C

362. Which Latin American nation lost Panama to a U.S.-backed revolution after it refused to bend to U.S. demands in the construction of a canal there?

(A) Venezuela
(B) Guatemala
(C) Honduras
(D) Colombia

363. In which Latin American nation did indigenous people play the most prominent political role during and after the winning of independence?

(A) Argentina
(B) Colombia
(C) Brazil
(D) Mexico

364. Which statement best characterizes Ottoman and Qing Chinese relations with the West by about 1750?

(A) Both empires were in full military retreat and subject to carrying out Western economic demands.
(B) Both empires were successfully carrying out policies of isolation from the West.
(C) Qing China was able to strongly regulate relations with the West while Ottoman rulers were less able to repel Western incursions into their territorial waters.
(D) Qing China pursued a policy of imitation of Western industrial and mercantile practices while Ottoman rulers refused to do so.

365. A long period of Ottoman territorial retreat ended with the birth of which modern nation?

(A) Iran
(B) Pakistan
(C) Turkey
(D) Egypt

366. Initial expansion of Western-style university systems, communication methods, railways, and newspaper production and the promulgation of a European-style constitution are associated with which period in the history of the Ottoman Empire?

(A) World War I era
(B) Era of Suleyman the Magnificent
(C) Great Depression era
(D) Tanzimat reform era

367. The nineteenth-century Egyptian political leader Muhammad Ali is best known for

(A) Revitalization of Islamic fundamentalism in the Ottoman world

(B) Defeat of the British navy to prevent Greek independence

(C) Determined but ultimately unsuccessful efforts to modernize Egypt's economy along Western lines

(D) Breaking Egyptian dependence on cotton exports in trade relations

368. Which of the following made Egypt an attractive target for Western imperialist expansion in the late nineteenth century?

(A) Gold deposits

(B) Control of Nile River trade

(C) Lucrative tourism prospects

(D) Construction and control of the Suez Canal

369. Which of the following does not belong in a list of policies generally followed by a rising Chinese dynasty?

(A) Repair and expansion of dams, canals, and roads

(B) Lowering tax burdens for the peasantry

(C) Expanding opportunities for peasants to own land

(D) Concentration of land ownership into ever fewer hands

370. Which of the following best describes China's trade relations with the rest of the world by about 1750?

(A) Export of Chinese manufactured and luxury goods in exchange for Western manufactured and luxury goods

(B) Export of Chinese manufactured and luxury goods in exchange for silver

(C) Import of Western manufactured and luxury goods in exchange for silver

(D) Negligible levels of trade with the rest of the world since China produced all it needed

371. Which of the following does NOT belong in a list of nineteenth-century challenges to the rule of the Qing dynasty in China?

(A) Floods
(B) Peasant rebellion
(C) Foreign invasion
(D) Expanding infl uence of communism in China

372. Which statement best captures the ruling Qing dynasty's attitude toward the West particularly in the period before the Opium Wars?

(A) Western civilization possessed military and industrial practices worthy of emulation.
(B) Western civilization posed a mortal threat to Chinese civilization.
(C) Western civilization was just another barbarian foreign society.
(D) Western civilization possessed artistic and intellectual practices worthy of emulation.

373. Which of the following best explains the reason the British turned to trading opium in China?

(A) Firsthand experience supplying mass opium addiction in the thirteen colonies proved the profitability of the trade.
(B) British merchants could find no other commodity the Chinese needed.
(C) Successful expansion of the opium trade in India provided a model for replication.
(D) Imperialist designs for direct rule in China would be more easily attainable over a population pacified by narcotics.

374. Land redistribution, reforms to simplify Chinese writing, equality for women, and armed struggle were major features of which pair of Chinese movements?

(A) Taiping Rebellion, Communist
(B) May Fourth Movement, Taiping Rebellion
(C) Nationalist, Taiping Rebellion
(D) May Fourth Movement, Communist

375. Which does NOT belong in a group of nations that had achieved territorial concessions in China by 1914?

(A) Japan
(B) Germany
(C) Britain
(D) Italy

376. Which of the following does NOT belong in a list of Chinese movements resentful of foreign domination?

(A) Boxer Rebellion
(B) May Fourth Movement
(C) Tanzimat Reform Movement
(D) Chinese Communist Movement

377. Which of the following is NOT a reason Chinese civilization suffered a more total collapse in the face of Western pressure than Muslim civilization had by 1914?

(A) Muslims had faced conflict with the West since the birth of their religion and hence were more accustomed to it, while the shock of Western interference was more abrupt for the Chinese.
(B) Muslims were not bound to defend a single state, while the Chinese destiny was linked to the survival of the Qing dynasty.
(C) Muslim civilization was concentrated in a more densely populated and urbanized manner and better suited to coastal or naval defense than the more rural and inland Chinese population.
(D) Muslim rulers were somewhat accustomed to exchange of knowledge with the West while the Chinese elites tended to view outsiders as barbarians one and all.

378. Which Chinese imperial bureaucrat wrote a famous letter to Queen Victoria demanding a cessation of British shipment of opium into China?

(A) Lin Zexu
(B) Qianlong
(C) Sun Yat-sen
(D) Pu Yi

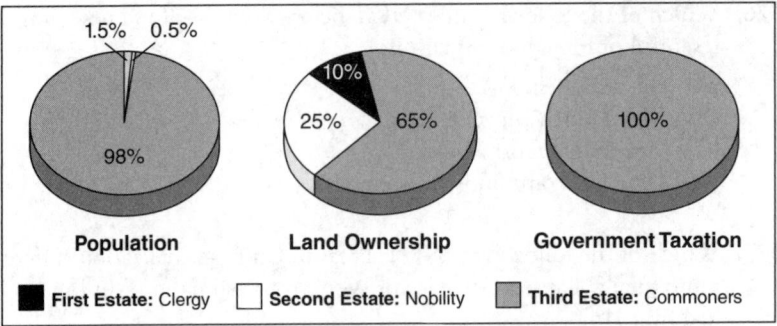

Source: Jackson J. Spielvogel, *World History*, Glencoe/McGraw-Hill, 2003 (adapted)

379. The pie charts above are best understood in the context of

(A) Conditions that led to the French Revolution
(B) European practice of slavery in France
(C) Industrial Revolution effects on workers
(D) Patriarchy in pre-Revolutionary France

380. As seen in the pie charts above question 379, compared to the American Revolution, the French Revolution

(A) Had less impact on the world's supply of cotton and tobacco
(B) Was also brought about by the poor conditions of the bourgeoisie
(C) Was a social upheaval as well as a political revolution
(D) Led to the rise of a military general who ruled as dictator

By the late eighteenth century the French colony at San-Domingue had become the largest producer of arguably the New World's most important commodity—sugar. Loss of this colony to the "excesses" of liberty that the French Revolution had inspired among the enslaved population on that island was intolerable to the ruling classes that emerged in France by the turn of the nineteenth century. In May 1802, Napoleon's force tried to reestablish slavery in Haiti. Toussaint L'Ouverture, leader of the Haitian Revolution, was kidnapped and deported back to France. The effect was to enrage the black majority and provoke even greater rebellion. By now black soldiers had gained experience in organizing an army. The French were at a disadvantage, they were more susceptible to disease (particularly yellow fever) than their opponents and reinforcements were difficult to obtain from France. The French troops were also demoralized by fighting against enemies who sang La Marseillaise and invoked revolutionary ideas. One officer, Lacroix, asked, "Have our barbarous enemies justice on their side? Are we no longer the soldiers of Republican France? And have we become the crude instruments of policy?"

381. The secondary source above supports which of the following conclusions?

   (A) French soldiers sent to Haiti had more immunity to disease than Haitians fighting for their homeland.

   (B) Napoleon's soldiers sent Toussaint L'Ouverture back to Haiti where he died of yellow fever.

   (C) British and French soldiers fought together to end slavery in the Americas as a whole.

   (D) Some French soldiers in Haiti questioned the incompatibility of their mission with Republican values.

382. Which factor had the LEAST impact on creating the conditions that gave rise to the situation described in the passage?

   (A) The French island colony of Haiti was extremely valuable for France because of its sugar crop.

   (B) Slavery was first established in Santo Domingue/Haiti in the early 1700s by French traders and settlers.

   (C) French revolutionary ideas such as equality and democracy began to spread to Haiti by 1790.

   (D) The British anti-slavery movement was established by the Quaker and Evangelical Christian community.

FIGURES ON NATIONALITIES WITHIN THE OTTOMAN EMPIRE

Ethnic Group (Total Population) Percentage of Empire	Subgroup	Subgroup Population
Turkish group (14,020,000) 49.1%	Ottoman Turks	13,500,000
	Turkomans	300,000
	Tatars	220,000
Greco-Latin group (3,520,000) 12.3%	Greeks	2,100,000
	Kutzo-Vlachs	220,000
	Albanians	1,200,000
Slavic group (4,550,000) 15.9%	Serbo-Croatians	1,500,000
	Bulgarians	3,000,000
	Cossacks	32,000
	Lipovans	18,000
Georgian group (1,020,000) 3.6%	Circassians	1,000,000
	Lazes	20,000
Indian group (212,000) 0.7%	Gypsies	212,000
Persian group (3,620,000) 12.7%	Armenians	2,500,000
	Kurds	1,000,000
	Druze, Mutawalis, Nusayris, and Yazidis	120,000
Semites (1,611,000) 5.6%	Jews	158,000
	Arabs	1,000,000
	Syrian-Chaldaeans	160,000
	Maronites	293,000

Total Population of the Ottoman Empire, 1876: 28,553,000

383. The series of reforms around the mid-nineteenth century that put all Ottomans, regardless of religion or ethnicity, on an equal footing legally was called

(A) The 100 Days of Reform
(B) The Tanzimat Reforms
(C) The Meiji Reforms
(D) The Dhimmi Reforms

384. By the end of the nineteenth century, which of the following was a result of the Ottoman division of its subjects by ethnicity and region?

(A) A rise in nationalism among the empire's ethnicities
(B) Calls for the creation of a worker-led state
(C) A migration of peoples to the Americas from Eurasia
(D) The expansion of the Ottoman Empire in Asia

Woodblock print of Yokohama kaigan tetsudō jōkisha no zu, *Picture of a Steam Locomotive along the Yokohama Waterfront.* Artist: Hiroshige III (1842–1894), c. 1874.

385. Which of the following events was most important in creating the economic conditions illustrated in the image above?

(A) The Tokugawa Shogun's decision to isolate itself from the world in 1613
(B) U.S. Navy commodore Matthew Perry's visit to Tokyo Bay in 1853
(C) The Chinese acceptance of the Treaty of Nanking in 1842 to open more trade ports
(D) The Japanese seizure of Korea and Taiwan in the Sino-Japanese war in 1895

386. Compared to the changes in Japan shown in the image above question 385, by the late nineteenth century China

(A) Largely did not reform its society and economy
(B) Surpassed Japan in reforming its society and economy
(C) Had still not opened its nation to foreign trade and influence
(D) Had only reformed its economy but not its politics or society

387. The Japanese woodblock print above question 386 was produced in a domestic system with specialized labor with a breakdown of labor tasks. This was part of a Japanese tradition that stretched back to before the Tokugawa era. Which of the following therefore is true?

(A) Japan's belief system had switched to the monotheistic faith of Christianity.
(B) Japan's artistic tradition had long surpassed the West in its use of colors and detail.
(C) Japan's society held merchants and craftsmen in the highest regard and status.
(D) Japan's modernization had some antecedents before the encounter with the West in 1853.

Luddites smashing a power loom in 1812

388. The Luddite movement of early nineteenth-century England is best seen as

(A) A reaction to the Industrial Revolution
(B) A reaction to Communist ideology
(C) Supporters of Social Darwinism
(D) A reaction to population increases

389. How did Karl Marx suggest the workers ought to resolve the conflict captured in the image above?

(A) Return to life as a rural peasant and take up subsistence farming similar to life before industrialization
(B) Continue their efforts to smash the machines and return the economy to the era of small-scale handicraft production
(C) Take up arms, establish rule of the proletariat, and institute public ownership of the means of production
(D) Cooperate with industrial capitalists to boost efficiency and output for the benefit of the state

China: The Cake of Kings . . . and Emperors, in *Le Petit Journal,* January 16, 1898

390. Which of the following contributed most directly to the condition depicted in the cartoon above?

(A) China's isolation from the rest of the world
(B) China's military weakness compared to the West
(C) China's dynastic cycle guaranteed transition to a ruling elite capable of halting Western imperial designs on China
(D) China's trade imbalance with Japan and the West

391. China's condition in the cartoon above question 390 is best compared to the situation in which of the following areas of the world in the late nineteenth and early twentieth centuries?

(A) Africa
(B) Western Europe
(C) United States of America
(D) Eastern Europe

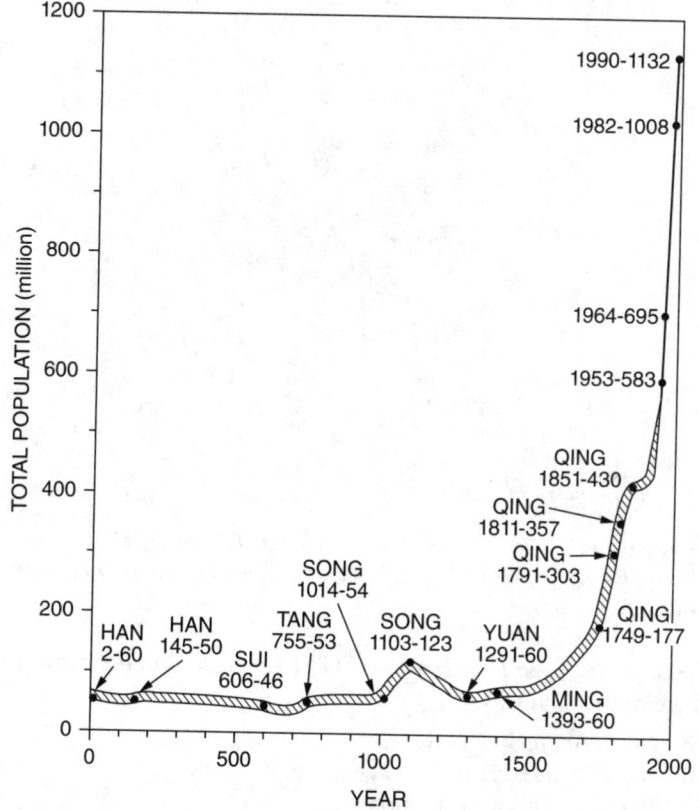

Chinese population 0 CE–2000 CE

392. Which of the following best supports a historical argument on the huge population growth illustrated in the chart during the Qing Dynasty from 1644 to 1911?

(A) New World crops
(B) Gunpowder technology
(C) Domestication of animals
(D) Silk Road trade

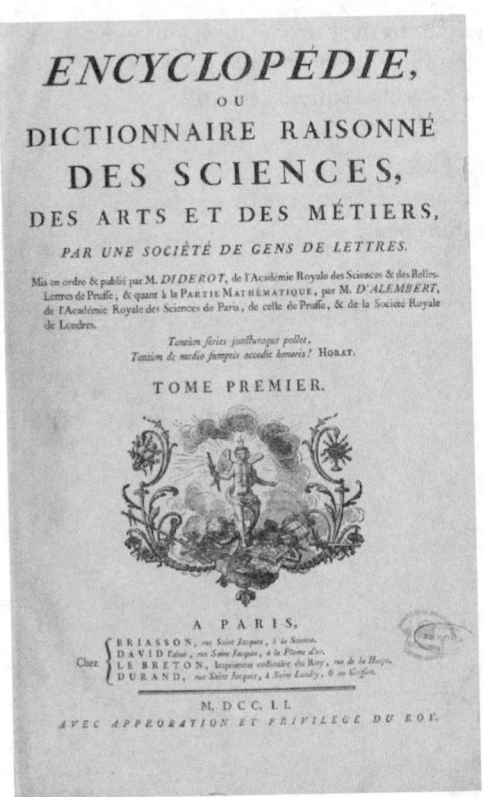

Cover page of the *Encyclopedia or a Systematic Dictionary of the Sciences, Arts and Crafts*, edited by Denis Diderot and Jean le Rond D'Alembert, printed in 1751

393. The printing of the *Encyclopedia* in 1751 is best seen in the context of which of the following?

(A) The Glorious Revolution
(B) The Enlightenment
(C) The Copernican Revolution
(D) The Inquisition

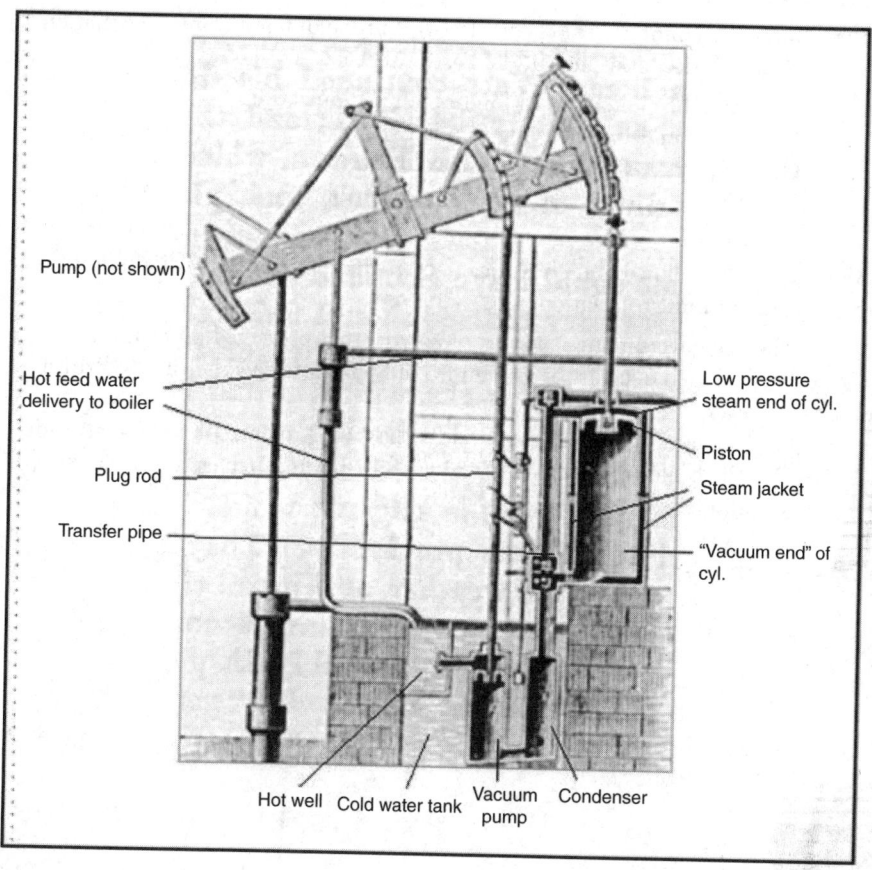

Schematic of James Watt's steam engine, 1878

394. The image above showing James Watt's steam engine was a result of which of the following historical events and processes?

(A) The practical application of science in technology
(B) The Enlightenment thought on natural rights
(C) The development of iron and bronze technology
(D) The Colombian Exchange of plants and animals

395. In the early modern era (1750–1914), Europe differed from the situation in Asia, Africa, and the Middle East in that it

(A) Launched an era of exploration and colonization
(B) Began a decline in living standards
(C) Erupted in world wars plus a cold war
(D) Led the world in the Industrial Revolution

396. All of the following are historical factors that help explain Britain's role as a leader of industrialization EXCEPT

(A) The government's support of patents that protected innovation
(B) The rich deposits of iron and coal lying close together in the British Isles
(C) The lack of an educated middle class with an entrepreneurial attitude
(D) The building of transportation infrastructure such as roads, canals, and later railroads

From this date to the end of the Terror, twenty-three months later, the story of the relations between the Revolution and the Church, though wild and terrible, is simple: it is a story of mere persecution culminating in extremes of cruelty and in the supposed uprooting of Christianity in France. The orthodox clergy were everywhere regarded by this time as the typical enemies of the revolutionary movement; they themselves regarded the revolutionary movement, by this time, as being principally an attempt to destroy the Catholic Church. There followed immediately a general attack upon religion. . . . The attempt at mere "de-christianisation," as it was called, failed, but the months of terror and cruelty, the vast number of martyrdoms (for they were no less) and the incredible sufferings and indignities to which the priests who attempted to remain in the country were subjected . . . . Conversely, the picture of the priest, . . . as the fatal and necessary opponent of the revolutionary theory, became so fixed in the mind of the Republican that two generations did nothing to eliminate it, and that even in our time the older men, in spite of pure theory, cannot rid themselves of an imagined connection between the Catholic Church and an international conspiracy against democracy. Nor does this non-rational but very real feeling lack support from the utterances of those who, in opposing the political theory of the French Revolution, consistently quote the Catholic Church as its necessary and holy antagonist.

Source: Hilaire Belloc, *The French Revolution,* 1911

397. The reading above can be understood best in the context of which of the following statements about the French Revolution?

(A) The Catholic Church was seen as one of the pillars of the Old Regime and a natural enemy of political change.

(B) The Catholic Church was an all-powerful institution in Europe and had retained all of its power since the Middle Ages.

(C) The Revolutionaries tried to ally themselves with the Catholic Church due to its belief in social justice and anti-hierarchal stance.

(D) The French Revolution opposed the spreading of the Catholic faith as foreign to its native Jewish belief system.

398. The reading above question 397 is written from the historical perspective of which of the following authors?

(A) A French Catholic

(B) An Italian Anarchist

(C) A French Revolutionary

(D) An American sailor

I think I may fairly make two postulata. First, That food is necessary to the existence of man. Secondly, That the passion between the sexes is necessary, and will remain nearly in its present state. . . . Assuming then my postulata as granted, I say, that the power of population is indefinitely greater than the power in the earth to produce subsistence for man. Population, when unchecked, increases in a geometrical ratio. Subsistence increases only in an arithmetical ratio. A slight acquaintance with numbers will shew the immensity of the first power in comparison of the second. By that law of our nature which makes food necessary to the life of man, the effects of these two unequal powers must be kept equal. This implies a strong and constantly operating check on population from the difficulty of subsistence. This difficulty must fall somewhere; and must necessarily be severely felt by a large portion of mankind.

Source: Thomas Malthus. *An Essay on the Principle of Population,*
Chapter I, 1798

399. Based on the reading above, Thomas Malthus in his famous piece is warning of which problem?

(A) Depopulation
(B) War and conflict
(C) Overpopulation
(D) Sexual transmitted disease

400. Which of the following historical processes most closely bears out the thesis Malthus put forward?

(A) The Green Revolution
(B) The Irish Potato Famine
(C) The American Civil War
(D) The Trans-Atlantic Migration

CHAPTER 5

The Present Era: 1914 to Present

Controlling Idea: An "Age of Extremes"

Dr. Eric Hobsbawm (Emeritus Professor at Birkbeck College, University of London and the New School in New York City) titled his excellent book on the "short twentieth century," 1914–1991, the *Age of Extremes*, and this phrase is a useful way to begin to conceptualize the dizzying scope and pace of change we have seen in the years since the opening shots of the First World War in 1914. Where before we had wars now we have had world wars. Where before we had powers now we have seen superpowers. The explosion of technological innovation and productive capacity we saw in the Industrial Revolution has been expanded upon in ways individuals alive in 1914 could scarcely dream of. Yet all too familiar, in point of fact ancient, patterns of poverty still define life for billions of people. It is, then, an "Age of Extremes" in wealth and poverty and an "Age of Extremes" for the biosphere where we have reached the situation in which man-made gases contribute to planetary climate change.

401. Which of the following best characterizes developments in the societies of Western Europe in the decades after World War II?
  I. Expanding welfare state provisions
  II. Steady economic growth
  III. Broad enthusiasm for expansion of colonial holdings
  (A) I only
  (B) I and II
  (C) I and III
  (D) II only

402. Which political system, discredited by its inability to effectively prevent economic collapse or a turn to political extremism, emerged triumphant in the post–World War II West?

(A) Socialism
(B) Liberal democracy
(C) Fascism
(D) Monarchy

403. Which nation emerged as the preeminent force in the West after World War II?

(A) England
(B) France
(C) United States
(D) West Germany

404. Which of the following phrases is most closely associated with the guarantee of U.S. protection from Soviet aggression offered to Western Europe and Japan during the Cold War era?

(A) Détente
(B) Nuclear umbrella
(C) Isolationism
(D) Berlin airlift

405. The North Atlantic Treaty Organization (NATO) and the Warsaw Pact are most accurately described as
  I. Free trade zones
 II. Collective security organizations
III. Colonial holdings

(A) I and II
(B) II and III
(C) I and III
(D) II only

406. Nikita Khrushchev is best known for

(A) Repudiation of repressive measures taken during the Stalin era
(B) Abandonment of Five-Year Plans and collective farms
(C) Glasnost
(D) Starving Soviet scientists of resources necessary to match Western achievements

407. Which socialist Eastern European nation was not a Soviet satellite state?

(A) Romania
(B) Hungary
(C) East Germany
(D) Yugoslavia

408. Which of the following was NOT a characteristic of the Soviet economy after World War II?

(A) Source of massive environmental damage
(B) Generally unresponsive to demand for consumer goods
(C) Incapable of significant arms production
(D) Centrally planned

409. Which U.S. general is most closely associated with a program of economic assistance to Western European nations struggling to rebuild after World War II?

(A) Adlai Stevenson
(B) Dwight Eisenhower
(C) George Patton
(D) George Marshall

410. In which of the following cases did the United States provide aid to break a Soviet blockade?

(A) U-2 incident
(B) Bay of Pigs invasion
(C) Berlin airlift
(D) Marshall Plan

411. The United States imposed all of the following elements on Japanese state and society after World War II EXCEPT

(A) Separation of legislative and executive powers
(B) Strict secular government, banning Shintoism as state religion
(C) Land reform
(D) Banning labor unions

412. On what continent did the United States fight its two largest conflicts of the Cold War era?

(A) Europe
(B) Asia
(C) Africa
(D) Australia

413. Which was true of both the Korean War and the Vietnam War?
  I. During the war the United States fought a communist North from base areas in a U.S.-friendly South.
  II. U.S. opponents received direct aid from the USSR and/or China.
  III. U.S. forces operated under a UN mandate.

(A) I and II
(B) II and III
(C) I and III
(D) II only

414. Which was true of the Korean War but not the Vietnam War?
  I. Conflict resulted in a lasting U.S. occupation.
  II. Conflict resulted in unification of North and South under communist rule.
  III. U.S. commanding officers argued for the use of nuclear weapons against the enemy.

(A) I and II
(B) II and III
(C) I and III
(D) II only

415. Mao's campaign to infuse industrial development into the national economy at the commune level was called

(A) New Democracy
(B) Protracted Warfare
(C) "Hundred Flowers" Period
(D) The Great Leap Forward

416. Which formerly colonized country has taken the most drastic measures to limit population growth?

(A) Mexico
(B) Nigeria
(C) India
(D) China

417. The "Great Revolution for a Proletarian Culture" in China is best described as

(A) A massive Deng Xiaoping–era program for technical training of peasants in industrial techniques

(B) The strategic retreat during the 1930s led by Mao Zedong from southern China to base areas to the north and west

(C) A 1960s–era campaign where mass mobilizations of youth were employed to target and repress "capitalist roaders" in positions of authority and continue the violent revolutionary struggle for a communist society

(D) Student demonstrations for political reform in 1989 brutally suppressed by Chinese authorities

418. Which of the following is NOT among the "Four Modernizations" put forward by Deng Xiaoping as key to economic self-reliance and emergence of China as a world power by the early twenty-first century?

(A) Agriculture

(B) Industry

(C) Science and technology

(D) Classless society

419. Which of the following best characterizes developments in China since 1979?

  I. Massive internal migration

 II. Strong export-driven economic growth

III. Multiparty elections

(A) I and II

(B) II and III

(C) I and III

(D) II only

420. Neocolonialism is best defined as

(A) Western efforts to expand colonial holdings after the Second World War

(B) The ongoing situation of economic dependency that afflicts "Third World" even after decolonization

(C) The post–World War II population boom in "Third World"

(D) A description of the Soviet relationship with satellite states of Eastern Europe during the Cold War

421. Which is an impact of population growth in the developing world?

(A) Declining importance of the International Monetary Fund in the global economy
(B) Falling numbers of refugees
(C) Rapid and haphazard urbanization
(D) Rising status for females

422. Which goal did nationalist leaders find most difficult to achieve upon gaining independence?

(A) Economic development and jobs for all
(B) Maintenance of territorial integrity of the new nations
(C) Participation in world trade
(D) Membership in the United Nations

423. Which was the most typical response of nationalist leaders in developing countries to popular unrest connected to persistent poverty and/or ethnic strife?

(A) Requests for the return of Western colonial management
(B) A turn to military dictatorship
(C) Free and fair elections of new leaders capable of resolving major grievances
(D) Establishment of new international borders to appease minority ethnicities

424. Who was the leader of the first sub-Saharan nation to gain independence?

(A) Jomo Kenyatta
(B) Nelson Mandela
(C) Gamal Abdel Nasser
(D) Kwame Nkrumah

425. Which of the following is NOT a trend or event associated with developments in post–WWII Egypt?

(A) Expulsion of the British from the Suez Canal Zone
(B) Construction of the Aswan dam
(C) Growth of Islamic fundamentalism
(D) Successful import-substitution industrialization

426. Which of the following accurately summarizes developments in India since independence?

   I. Maintenance of civilian rule and representative democracy

   II. Growth of a middle class and information technology sector

   III. Elimination of caste distinctions

   IV. Penetration of Green Revolution agricultural techniques down to the village level

   (A) I and IV

   (B) II and III

   (C) I, II, and III

   (D) I, II, and IV

427. Which of the following statements about the Iranian Revolution of 1979 is most accurate?

   (A) It marked the end of British colonialism in Iran.

   (B) It overthrew a monarchy and installed a liberal democracy.

   (C) It was guided by a non-Western ideology.

   (D) It drew its main ideological inspiration from the teachings of Karl Marx.

428. Which of the following was the only newly independent nation to experience civil war secession and the formation of another nation within decades of decolonization?

   (A) Sudan

   (B) South Africa

   (C) Mexico

   (D) Pakistan

429. Which natural resource or crop have developing nations been able to trade in the global economy on terms most favorable to themselves?

   (A) Cocoa

   (B) Coffee

   (C) Oil

   (D) Diamonds

430. Why was South Africa's independence struggle atypical when compared with most other African nations?

(A) Few other African nations gained independence in the 1960s.

(B) South Africa embarked on a program of rapid state-directed industrialization soon after achieving independence.

(C) Independence was negotiated by a South African government that consisted of white settlers only.

(D) South Africa nationalized gold and diamond mines and directed profits from their operation into development projects to lift the standard of living of the black majority there.

431. Nelson Mandela and Steven Biko are associated with the struggle against what?

(A) Soviet socialism

(B) South African apartheid

(C) U.S. imperialism

(D) French colonialism

432. Which West African nation boasts the continent's largest population and substantial oil reserves?

(A) Senegal

(B) Ghana

(C) Ethiopia

(D) Nigeria

433. Which of the following was the first group targeted by the Nazis for repression once they seized power in Germany?

(A) Jews

(B) Communists

(C) Gypsies

(D) Homosexuals

434. Who was the first fascist dictator?

(A) Friedrich Nietzsche

(B) Adolf Hitler

(C) Benito Mussolini

(D) Vladimir I. Lenin

435. Which was the first twentieth-century revolutionary movement to successfully topple an existing regime?

(A) Iranian
(B) Chinese
(C) Mexican
(D) Russian

436. Which element of the Mexican revolutionary movement of 1910 represented the greatest continuity from nineteenth-century popular movements there?

(A) Vocal demands of the Catholic church for increased power
(B) Dependence on French military assistance in order to achieve regime change
(C) Prominent role played by mestizo and Indian elements demanding land reform
(D) International acclaim for artistic representatives of the movement such as Diego Rivera

437. Where in modern Europe has the rule of liberal democracy been most brief?

(A) France
(B) England
(C) Sweden
(D) Russia

438. Which of the following were the main slogans the Bolsheviks put forward on their road to power in 1917?

I. Peace
II. Communism
III. Land
IV. Bread

(A) I, II, and IV
(B) II, III, and IV
(C) I, II, and III
(D) I, III, and IV

439. Why did the Bolshevik regime turn to a New Economic Policy in the early 1920s?

(A) A centrally planned economy was seen as the next logical step after the "War Communism" system employed during the civil war.

(B) Lenin and leading Bolshevik elements gave up socialism as a long-range goal.

(C) Lenin and leading Bolshevik elements sought to bring back free enterprise and the profit motive in order to jump-start an economy severely dislocated by World War I and the Russian Civil War.

(D) Stalin had already replaced Lenin as leader of the Bolsheviks and sought a more rapid push toward communism.

440. How were minority ethnic groups of the old Russian Empire treated by the new Bolshevik regime?

(A) Most individuals belonging to minorities experienced forced deportation to Siberia.

(B) Minority groups were granted semiautonomous republics bound to pursuing a socialist course.

(C) Minority ethnicities were forcibly intermarried with ethnic Russians to breed them out of existence.

(D) All minority groups were granted "Soviet Socialist Republic" territory except for Jews.

441. Which political figure eventually emerged to lead the Bolshevik Party after the death of Lenin?

(A) Trotsky

(B) Khrushchev

(C) Gorbachev

(D) Stalin

442. Which factor in the Russian and Chinese revolutions was not present in the French Revolution?

(A) Rural unrest

(B) Urban discontent

(C) Military intervention by neighboring or outside powers

(D) The ideas of Karl Marx and Friedrich Engels

443. Where in the world did the Japanese most vigorously seek to achieve territorial expansion in the years following 1914?

(A) Korea

(B) Mongolia

(C) Indonesia

(D) China

444. Which development prompted Chinese nationalists and communists to suspend civil war and form a shaky common cause?

(A) Death of Sun Yat-sen

(B) Japanese invasion of China

(C) Massive American investment to build up industrial sectors in Chinese urban centers

(D) Communist long march to sanctuary in nationalist base areas in northwest China

445. Which of the following statements about Western economies in the 1920s are generally accepted by historians as factors causing the Great Depression?

   I. Overproduction in industry and especially agriculture

  II. Unsustainable borrowing, lending, and stock market speculation

 III. Strong government regulation of industry

(A) I and II

(B) II and III

(C) I and III

(D) II only

446. Which of the following answer choices places the events associated with the Great Depression in the United States in proper chronological order?

   I. Bank failures

  II. October 1929 stock market crash

 III. Skyrocketing unemployment

 IV. New Deal programs implemented by FDR

(A) I, II, III, IV

(B) III, I, II, IV

(C) IV, III, II, I

(D) II, I, III, IV

447. Why were Great Britain and France able to insulate themselves from the Great Depression to a greater extent than Germany or the United States?

(A) By 1929, industrial production was no longer central to their national economies.

(B) Both nations unloaded a certain amount of surplus industrial production on markets in their extensive colonial holdings.

(C) Strong labor movements in both countries refused to accept layoffs.

(D) Britain and France were able to collect on loans made to Germany.

448. In which nation did parliamentary democracy survive the 1930s?

(A) Spain

(B) Germany

(C) France

(D) Brazil

449. Which of the following terms refers to the need and right of the German people to expand their territory according to Adolf Hitler?

(A) *Untermenschen*

(B) *Luftwaffe*

(C) *Lebensraum*

(D) *Wiener schnitzel*

450. Adolf Hitler wrote which book laying out his vision and program for Germany's rise to world supremacy?

(A) *State and Revolution*

(B) *The Communist Manifesto*

(C) *Mein Kampf*

(D) *Civilization and Its Discontents*

451. How was the Spanish Civil War different from World War II?

(A) In the Spanish Civil War, civilian populations were subjected to aerial bombing.

(B) In the Spanish Civil War, Soviet-supplied forces fought fascist armies on European soil while liberal democracies delayed action.

(C) In the Spanish Civil War, fascists emerged victorious.

(D) In the Spanish Civil War, industrial-era weaponry was employed.

452. Which global trend had a significant impact in Latin America in the 1930s and 1940s?

   I. Slumping demand for raw materials on world markets

  II. Growing influence of fascism

 III. Independence struggles in colonized regions

(A) I only

(B) I and II

(C) I and III

(D) II and III

453. Which policy course did Japanese and German governments take to reverse the economic difficulties of the 1930s?

(A) Stimulation of industry through war preparation

(B) Provision of social insurance through liberal democratic parliamentary means

(C) Worker control of industry

(D) Laissez-faire approach toward economic policy

454. Which element of German fascism was NOT also found in 1930s Japan?

(A) Suspension of parliamentary authority

(B) Ideology of racial supremacy

(C) State-sanctioned mob violence against ethnic minorities

(D) Annexation of nearby territory

455. Which term do historians employ to describe both Hitler's Germany and Stalin's USSR?

(A) Fascist

(B) Communist

(C) Totalitarian

(D) Democratic

456. Which of the following were offered by the Stalin regime as reasons to pursue collectivization of agriculture and Five-Year Plans in industry after 1928?

    I. Reversal of the NEP and inculcation of socialist habits among the Soviet masses

    II. Reduction of the Soviet population to environmentally sustainable levels

    III. Rapid industrialization to prepare for a second imperialist invasion of the USSR

(A) I only

(B) I and II

(C) II and III

(D) I and III

457. Which Soviet leader was a leading force in imposing economic, diplomatic, and political reforms after 1985 that contributed directly to the demise of Soviet socialism?

(A) Nikolay Bukharin

(B) Leonid Brezhnev

(C) Mikhail Gorbachev

(D) Nikita Khrushchev

458. Which best characterizes weaknesses of the Soviet economy after World War II?

    I. Inflexible central planning

    II. Low worker morale and productivity

    III. Raw-material shortages

(A) I and II

(B) II and III

(C) I and III

(D) I only

459. Which Latin American nation stood apart from a general trend away from authoritarian or military rule that had taken hold across the region by the 1990s?

(A) Argentina

(B) Chile

(C) The Dominican Republic

(D) Cuba

460. The growing integration of all the peoples of the planet into a single economic and political model and accelerating sharing of cultural symbols is termed

(A) Egalitarianism
(B) Simulacra
(C) Postmodernism
(D) Globalization

461. Which is the most popular and accessible method worldwide of accessing the efficiencies of a new "information economy"?

(A) Mobile phones
(B) Personal computers
(C) Local libraries
(D) Satellite television

462. Which is most accurate about Western economic interests overseas in the postcolonial era?
   I. They have been imposed through formal colonization of lands and peoples of the developing world.
   II. They are pursued by multinational corporations.
   III. They have dwindled to the point of insignificance.

(A) I and II
(B) II and III
(C) I only
(D) II only

463. U.S. forces have seen military action most frequently to which region in the post–Cold War era?

(A) Pacific Rim
(B) Latin America
(C) Middle East and Central Asia
(D) Western Europe

464. What was the nationality of the majority of September 11 hijackers?

(A) Iraqi
(B) Palestinian
(C) Saudi Arabian
(D) Afghan

465. How are the nations of Latin America unique within the "Third World"?

(A) They have struggled to emerge from a dependent role in the global economy.

(B) They have experienced civil war in the post–WWII era.

(C) They gained political independence in the nineteenth century, in general.

(D) They continue to use a language imposed by colonial administrators in internal state affairs.

466. Which of the following twentieth-century Latin American regimes survived CIA-supported efforts to bring them down?

I. Arbenz regime in Guatemala

II. Castro regime in Cuba

III. Allende regime in Chile

(A) I only

(B) II only

(C) III only

(D) I and III

467. Which independent developing-country regime entered what is best termed as a dependent economic relationship with the Soviet Union that lasted until the collapse of the USSR in the early 1990s?

(A) Ghana

(B) Egypt

(C) India

(D) Cuba

468. When compared with the case of Mexico in the years since World War II, the people of Cuba have experienced greater progress in each of the following EXCEPT:

(A) Job security

(B) Housing

(C) Literacy

(D) Emigration rights

469. How did local Catholic church leaders demonstrate sensitivity to demands of the poor for social justice in twentieth-century Latin America?

(A) Demanding special infusions of charity from the Vatican that wiped out poverty in their parishes
(B) Formulation of a "liberation theology"
(C) Organization of sophisticated adoption schemes whereby the majority of children in poverty in Latin America were adopted by middle-class families in the West and sent to live there
(D) Renunciation of Christianity in favor of orthodox Marxist socialism

470. Which is the most common pattern of migration in the Americas today?

(A) From North America into Latin America
(B) From Latin American countryside to Latin American cities
(C) From Latin American cities into the Latin American countryside
(D) From Latin America into North America

471. Which of the following nations did not succumb to military rule in the post–WWII era?

(A) Bolivia
(B) Mexico
(C) El Salvador
(D) Argentina

472. Which Latin American nation faced some of the first major U.S. military action overseas of the post–Cold War era?

(A) Cuba
(B) Venezuela
(C) Haiti
(D) Panama

473. The United States pursued its interests in Latin America after World War II in all of the following forms EXCEPT

(A) Direct annexation
(B) Covert action to overthrow regimes perceived to be Soviet friendly
(C) Diplomatic pressure in international organizations
(D) Peace Corps presence

474. NAFTA has more closely integrated the economies of Canada, the United States, and

(A) Russia
(B) China
(C) Mexico
(D) Venezuela

475. Which of the following periods have been grouped together by world historians into a time called an "Age of Catastrophe" lasting from 1914 to 1945?

(A) World War I, Great Depression, Cold War
(B) Napoleonic Wars, World War I, World War II
(C) World War I, Great Depression, World War II
(D) World War II, Cold War, post–Cold War era

476. Which of the following trends were seen in the twentieth century?

(A) Rise and fall of communism and political independence for the former colonies
(B) Rise and fall of communism and the eradication of global poverty
(C) Eradication of global poverty and the onset of human-induced climate change
(D) Slowed population growth in industrialized regions and uninterrupted economic growth

477. Which of the following does NOT belong in a list of major impacts of the First World War?

(A) Bolshevik Revolution in Russia
(B) Rise of the United States and Japan
(C) Birth of the League of Nations
(D) Rise of nationalist sentiment in colonized regions of the globe

478. Where did white rule persist longest on the African continent?

(A) Rhodesia
(B) South Africa
(C) Angola
(D) Nigeria

Indian soldiers in the British armed forces in
World War I trenches in France, 1915

479. The image above is best understood in the context of

(A) The global nature of World War I due to imperialism
(B) The division of the world into Muslim and non-Muslim
(C) The spread of nationalist sentiment before World War I
(D) The ending of nonviolent protest among Indians

480. The image above question 479 depicts trench warfare during World War I. The use of this tactic in war was a result of which of the following conditions?

(A) Social Darwinism
(B) Transatlantic travel
(C) The Industrial Revolution
(D) Coal mining

481. By comparison, World War I differed from World War II in which of the following ways?

(A) World War II was a more limited geographical conflict.
(B) World War II involved a more mobile type of warfare.
(C) World War II was less destructive in terms of civilians.
(D) World War II resulted in a period of stability in China.

"It is no use for you to argue," Talaat answered, "we have already disposed of three quarters of the Armenians; there are none at all left in Bitlis, Van, and Erzeroum. The hatred between the Turks and the Armenians is now so intense that we have got to finish with them. If we don't, they will plan their revenge." "If you are not influenced by humane considerations," I replied, "think of the material loss. These people are your business men. They control many of your industries. They are very large tax-payers. What would become of you commercially without them?" "We care nothing about the commercial loss," replied Talaat. "We have figured all that out and we know that it will not exceed five million pounds. We don't worry about that. I have asked you to come here so as to let you know that our Armenian policy is absolutely fixed and that nothing can change it. We will not have the Armenians any-where in Anatolia. They can live in the desert but nowhere else."

I still attempted to persuade Talaat that the treatment of the Armenians was destroying Turkey in the eyes of the world, and that his country would never be able to recover from this infamy. "You are making a terrible mistake," I said, and I repeated the statement three times. "Yes, we may make mistakes," he replied, "but"—and he firmly closed his lips and shook his head—"we never regret."

Source: Henry Morgenthau's conversation with Mehmed Talaat, the Turkish Minister of the Interior in 1915 during World War I

482. The situation in the reading above is clear evidence of which of the following conclusions?

(A) Turkish elites were financially supportive of Armenian immigration to South or North America.

(B) Turkish elites were rightly concerned about economic repercussions that would follow their actions.

(C) Turkish elites were motivated by a feeling of scientific superiority that placed the Armenians as subhuman.

(D) Turkish elites knowingly committed acts of genocide against a minority ethnic group within their empire.

483. Which of the following long-term causes most directly led to the actions described in the reading above question 482?

(A) New technology being used to develop deadlier weapons

(B) The formation of the Triple Entente Alliance system

(C) Rising nationalism among various ethnic groups

(D) The European Mandate system in the Middle East

Source: 1930s era mural in the town hall of the Mexican city of Valladolid, 2014. (Photo by Sean McManamon.)

484. The causes of the Mexican Revolution of 1910 to 1920 were mainly based on which of the following?

(A) The grievances of the poor and vulnerable

(B) The injuries done to the Catholic Church

(C) The spread of Bolshevik ideas from Russia

(D) The rise of Mexican nationalism

485. In comparison to the Chinese Revolution of 1910, the Mexican Revolution also

(A) Overthrew a long-ruling monarchial dynasty
(B) Was caused by anger over foreign domination
(C) Resulted from the sale and use of opium
(D) Led to the establishment of communism

EXTREMISTS' RISE TO POWER IN RUSSIA

From Outset of Revolution They Have Thwarted Efforts of Moderate Governments.

SAPPED KERENSKY'S RULE

Supported Premier Only When the Korniloff Movement Filled Them with Apprehension.

Source: *New York Times* headline. November 9, 1917

486. The issues referred to in the headlines above is best understood in the context of

(A) World War I
(B) The Russian Revolution
(C) The rise of fascism
(D) The Great Depression

487. It can plausibly be argued that the seizure of power in Russia by radical socialists and communists in 1917 marks the beginning of

(A) The Mandate System
(B) The Cold War
(C) World War I
(D) The League of Nations

488. Which demand of the Bolsheviks had the least popular support at the time of their seizure of power in November of 1917?

(A) Peace
(B) Land
(C) Bread
(D) Communism

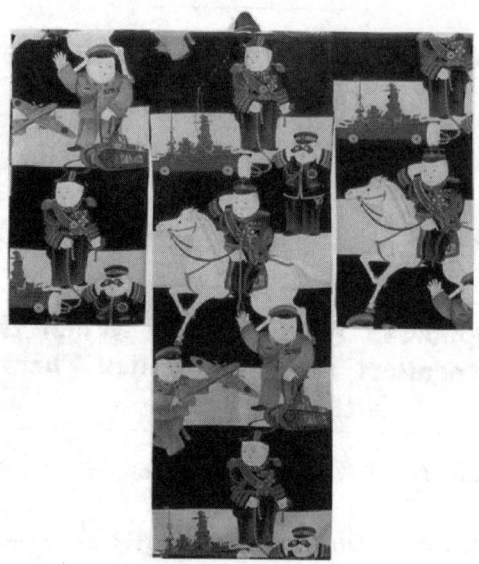

Boy's kimono with design from Japan,
c. late 1930s

489. The kimono shown above shows clear evidence of which of the following political attitudes prevalent among many Japanese people in the 1930s?

(A) Communism
(B) Industrialism
(C) Militarism
(D) Pacifism

490. The national sentiments expressed in the Japanese boy's kimono shown above question 489 are similar to

(A) Those found among the German public, specifically the youth, in Nazi Germany

(B) Those found among colonial elites chaffing under German domination

(C) Those expressed by the Indian Mohandas K. Gandhi during his Salt March

(D) The writings of the early League of Nations minutes and memorandum

Luedell Mitchell and Lavada Cherry in a Douglas Aircraft factory, United States, during World War II

491. The image shown above best demonstrates which of the following conclusions?

(A) Suffrage was granted to women for their participation in World War II.

(B) War-related factory work was the only job that women could acquire.

(C) Women were encouraged to take part in frontline combat positions.

(D) Total war requires the active involvement of the civilian population.

492. Which of the following was a direct result of the participation of African Americans and other nonwhite colonial peoples in Europe and Canada in World War II?

(A) A nonaligned stance during the Cold War
(B) A push for racial justice and civil rights
(C) Being suspected of communist sympathies
(D) A call for more environmental protections

Vietnamese Declaration of Independence

"All men are created equal. They are endowed by their Creator with certain inalienable rights; among these are Life, Liberty, and the pursuit of Happiness." This immortal statement was made in the Declaration of Independence of the United States of America in 1776. In a broader sense, this means: All the peoples on the earth are equal from birth, all the peoples have a right to live, to be happy and free. . . . we, members of the Provisional Government of the Democratic Republic of Vietnam, solemnly declare to the world that Vietnam has the right to be a free and independent country—and in fact is so already. The entire Vietnamese people are determined to mobilize all their physical and mental strength, to sacrifice their lives and property in order to safeguard their independence and liberty.

Source: The Vietnamese Declaration of Independence, which was read
by Ho Chi Minh in Hanoi on September 2, 1945

493. Which of the following statements are true of the Vietnamese Declaration of Independence shown above that was read out in the city of Hanoi on September 2, 1945?

(A) The intended audience was the Western powers, especially America, as much as it was the Vietnamese people.
(B) The Japanese reacted with fury and began to indiscriminately kill Vietnamese intellectuals and professionals.
(C) The Dutch colonial forces ignored the document and began preparations to regain their former colonial possession.
(D) The American president Harry Truman issued a strong statement of support for the Vietnamese nationalists.

494. The Vietnamese Declaration of Independence shows the clear influence of

(A) The Social Darwinist theories that portrayed Asians as inferior to Caucasians

(B) The nonviolent doctrine of *ahisma* that was used by Mohandas K. Gandhi in India

(C) Enlightenment principles that were similar to the American Declaration of Independence

(D) Fascist ideals enshrined in Benito Mussolini's 1932 article "What Is Fascism"

495. The reading above question 494 contradicts which of the following statements below concerning the Vietnamese independence movement in the post–World War II era?

(A) The Vietnamese desire for independence was in part a Moscow-directed effort to spread communism.

(B) The Vietnamese were too politically backward to understand modern concepts of government.

(C) The Vietnamese were a divided collection of ethnically and linguistically unrelated peoples.

(D) Vietnam was a southern province of China that sought reunification with China.

The Security Council,

- *Expressing its continuing concern with the grave situation in the Middle East,*

- *Emphasizing the inadmissibility of the acquisition of territory by war and the need to work for a just and lasting peace in which every State in the area can live in security,*

- *Emphasizing further that all Member States in their acceptance of the Charter of the United Nations have undertaken a commitment to act in accordance with Article 2 of the Charter,*

- *Affirms that the fulfillment of Charter principles requires the establishment of a just and lasting peace in the Middle East which should include the application of both the following principles:*

  1. *Withdrawal of Israeli armed forces from territories occupied in the recent conflict;*

  2. *Termination of all claims or states of belligerency and respect for and acknowledgement of the sovereignty, territorial integrity and political independence of every State in the area and their right to live in peace within secure and recognized boundaries free from threats or acts of force.*

Source: United Nations Resolution 242, November 22, 1967

496. The resolution above by the United Nations supports which of the following conclusions?
- (A) Israel in conjunction with Britain and France seized the Suez Canal from Egypt in 1956.
- (B) Nuclear proliferation in the Middle East is of the highest concern and must be approved by the Security Council.
- (C) The communal violence between Sunni and Shia Muslims must end and all land seized must be returned.
- (D) The lands (West Bank, Gaza Strip, and East Jerusalem) seized by Israel are not accepted by the world community.

497. The Arab-Israeli conflict has changed since United Nations Resolution 242 in all of the following ways EXCEPT from
- (A) Nationalist divisions to one of religious divisions
- (B) Wars between states to one of numerous terrorist acts
- (C) Small-scale guerilla war to one of devastating total war
- (D) Threats of conventional weapons to threats of nuclear weapons

Through our protective measures of 13 August 1961 we have only safeguarded and strengthened that frontier which was already drawn years ago and made into a dangerous front-line by the people in Bonn and West Berlin. How high and how strongly fortified a frontier must be, depends, as is common knowledge, on the kind of relations existing between the states of each side of the frontier. . . . We no longer wanted to stand by passively and see how doctors, engineers, and skilled workers were induced by refined methods unworthy of the dignity of man to give up their secure existence here and work in West Germany or West Berlin.

Source: 1962 brochure from the German Democratic Republic (GDR) published in English for foreign distribution

There are many people in the world who really don't understand, or say they don't, what is the great issue between the free world and the Communist world. Let them come to Berlin. There are some who say that communism is the wave of the future. Let them come to Berlin. Freedom has many difficulties and democracy is not perfect, but we have never had to put a wall up to keep our people in, to prevent them from leaving us. . . . Freedom is indivisible, and when one man is enslaved, all are not free. When all are free, then we can look forward to that day when this city will be joined as one and this country and this great Continent of Europe in a peaceful and hopeful globe. When that day finally comes, as it will, the people of West Berlin can take sober satisfaction in the fact that they were in the front lines for almost two decades. All free men, wherever they may live, are citizens of Berlin, and, therefore, as a free man, I take pride in the words "Ich bin ein Berliner."

Source: President John F. Kennedy's speech on June 26, 1963, when he visited Berlin

498. The second reading by President Kennedy differs from the first reading from the GDR in that it

(A) Takes a stand against illegal immigration to Berlin
(B) Agrees that the Berlin Wall is keeping the peace
(C) Opposes the Berlin Wall as antithetical to freedom
(D) Supports the communist idea of a divided Berlin

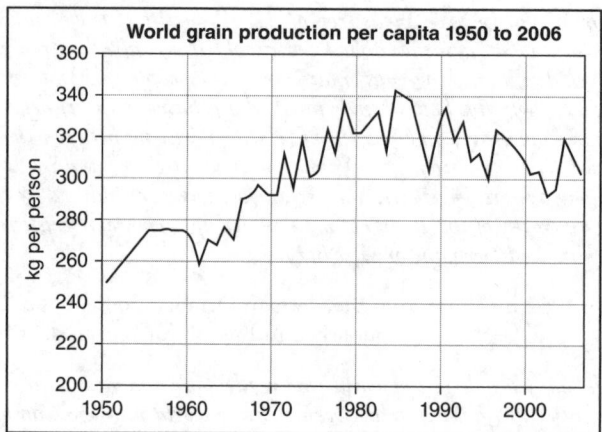

499. The Green Revolution was largely in response to which of the following developments in the postwar era?

(A) Tensions between the East and the West during the Cold War
(B) High population growth in the so-called Third World
(C) Increased use of science in weapons technology
(D) Spread of Old World foods to the New World

Source: Soviet propaganda poster issued in Uzbekistan, 1933,
"Strengthen working discipline in collective farms"

500. Based on the image above, the Soviet Union instituted which of the
following changes?

(A) The implementation of communist economic policies in rural areas
(B) The banishment of refugees from Central Asia to Eastern Europe
(C) The increase in population through centralized family planning
(D) The ending of payments to the old aristocracy from czarist Russia

ANSWERS

Chapter 1

1. (D) Civilization in this sense implies a level of complexity in social organization that requires a sedentary lifestyle.

2. (C) Sedentary agriculture emerges with the greatest ease in river valleys.

3. (D) Archaeologists have discovered the oldest evidence of civilization in the Tigris, Euphrates, and Nile River valleys, all of which belong to the greater Middle East region.

4. (C) The Sumerians settled into Mesopotamia (now modern Iraq). This is the earliest known civilization in the world and may also be referred to as the "cradle of civilization."

5. (D) Many portions of Hammurabi's Code make specific provisions based on the social class of the individuals involved. The passage provides no basis to make any other choice.

6. (D) No evidence supports the claim that the Chinese were involved with the building of the ancient Egyptian pyramids.

7. (D) Formidable mountain ranges and desert expanses separate the Chinese river valleys from the Middle East. However, archaeological evidence of long-distance trade connecting early Indus civilization and the Middle East has been found.

8. (C) This fact is reflected in the root of the word *phonics*, familiarity with which is key to reading.

9. (A) Writing was put to this purpose wherever it arose. Watch out for choice **(D)**; the Inca had no formal writing system but kept records by counting colored and knotted strings called *quipu*.

10. (A) *Perennial* means "growing once a year." Watch out for choice **(C)**; Mesoamerican civilization had no domesticated draft animals. Draft animals provide muscle power and include oxen, cows, and horses.

11. (A) Since Christianity and Islam are derived from Judaism, this makes Abraham an important historical figure to study.

12. (B) This characteristic is more widely recognized by Westerners in Confucian and Hindu traditions than in the Christian tradition. Numerous biblical passages exhort the poor and the slave to accept their lots in life and obey their masters. Choice **(A)** is false regarding Confucianism.

13. (B) Nile, Yellow, and Tigris-Euphrates valleys respectively; **(A)** is false for Shang China while choices **(C)** and **(D)** are false for both civilizations.

14. (C) Recreational use of gunpowder dates from the Song Dynasty (tenth to thirteenth centuries CE, roughly) with military application coming thereafter.

15. (A) Keep in mind the importance of the Greek navy in its rise to regional power.

16. (C) While monarchs before may have been limited by custom, historians date the emergence of constitutional monarchy to the British Isles in the centuries following the signing of the Magna Carta in the early thirteenth century.

17. (A) While the first and third bullet points are true for the Maya, the second one is not, making Harappan the only possible choice.

18. (A) The other civilizations on the list succumbed to human-induced shocks of war or peasant revolt. Less evidence for this persists to draw the same conclusion about the Indus River valley civilization.

19. (A) *Cultural diffusion* means "the spread of ideas or practices from one region to another," and this was evident with the Roman elite and their taste for silk garments.

20. (D) Construction of ships from metal required industrial techniques not developed until the nineteenth century when blast furnaces and the Bessemer process for creating steel were developed. Before the Industrial Revolution metalwork was limited to projects or items that could be produced by hand by a blacksmith.

21. (D) One of the great unsolved mysteries of the ancient world is that Harappan writing has not yet been deciphered.

22. (D) Cuneiform emerged in the Sumerian civilization. A pictograph is a simplified visual representation of an object in written form, an ideograph is a symbol that represents a concept, and phonetic symbols represent sounds. Cuneiform was a pictographic writing system.

23. (A) Archaeological excavation at all four sites reveal the earliest traces of monumental building, writing tablets, and urban living in the Tigris-Euphrates valley, where Sumerian civilization was born.

24. (D) Archaeological findings indicate that agriculture emerged roughly ten thousand years ago—long after *Homo erectus* had gone extinct by all available data.

25. (B) *Revolution* is a term applied to any abrupt shift in a course of human events that was sparked in a specific location or region. This question asks us to consider time frame. Political revolutions, such as the French or Russian revolution, tend to unfold more quickly, while nonpolitical revolutions (scientific, industrial) take place over a period of decades. Only the transition to sedentary agriculture took place over a period of centuries or even millennia.

26. (C) Paleolithic peoples had domesticated the wolf long before any "farm" animal. Choices **(A)** and **(D)** represent practices that died out, while choice **(B)** is not true of Paleolithic peoples.

27. (D) Sedentary society tended to give rise to social stratification, including slavery.

28. (B) Pastoral nomads established the viability of herding of animals as an economic activity; this viability continued through history until today.

29. (D) The "New World" refers to the Americas and the Western Hemisphere. Maize was an early crop that was unique to these civilizations.

30. (C) Large numbers of small children lessen the mobility of preagricultural nomadic groups; additionally, increased food output of agricultural production provided a basis for greater confinement of women of child-bearing age to the home.

31. (A) Biological and archaeological evidence supports this choice and none of the others.

32. (D) This is the basic model of early labor specialization. For choice **(C)**, archaeological digs of Paleolithic-era sites have revealed the presence of stone tools far from quarry locations, indicating long-distance trade was practiced. Choices **(A)** and **(B)** are false.

33. (B) Ailments such as chicken pox, swine flu, and bird flu in their very names indicate the propensity for pathogen sharing between people and domesticated animals. It also took awhile for plumbing to be invented. Sedentary peoples settled next to their pathogen-producing waste as well. Nomadic people never had to deal with these health hazards as they moved away from their wastes. All other choices are false.

34. (D) Genetic research supports the origin of anatomically modern humans in Africa, only.

35. (B) To some extent these three developments occurred simultaneously, but to the extent that one is a precondition for the next, this choice lays them out in correct order.

36. (D) Slash and burn requires the least manipulation of the natural world. Anthropological studies indicate that it is practiced by populations in a transitional phase between nomadic and agricultural practices.

37. (B) Radiocarbon dating of human remains, rock paintings (Australia in particular), and genetic studies all support this choice.

38. (D) Australian aborigines maintained a hunter-gatherer lifestyle until the continent was colonized by Westerners.

39. (D) *Neolithic* means "new stone age" and *paleolithic* means "old stone age." Neolithic has also become shorthand for "settled agricultural" and while some settled agriculturalists developed metal, preagricultural peoples generally did not for anything more than ornamental purposes.

40. (B) Hellas was the ancient name for Greece. *Hellenistic*, therefore, means "Greek-like" and dates from the spread of Greek culture along with the armies of Alexander, the greatest Greek empire builder.

41. (D) The rapid conquests of Alexander's armies fostered a Greek-directed sharing of ideas from the Indus River valley across the Middle East to the Mediterranean basin.

42. (D) This practice never changed; **(A)** and **(C)** were discontinued, and **(B)** never happened in any way that survives in the historical record.

43. (B) Based on fragmentary evidence, important reforms that lay the basis for Greek democracy date to the period of Solon's rule. Choices **(A)**, **(C)**, and **(D)** were philosophers.

44. (D) Athenian women experienced a highly cloistered lifestyle even in relation to other women in the ancient world.

45. (A) The Silk Roads connected these two civilizations. Scandinavia was more or less uncivilized while Polynesian and Olmec peoples were isolated by vast oceans. Gupta civilization had yet to exist in the days of classical Greek rule.

46. (D) Herodotus, sometimes called the "father of history," is not part of the chain of teaching that flowed from Socrates to Plato to Aristotle to Alexander.

47. (C) is accurate for both empires. Choices **(A)** and **(D)** are true for neither. Choice **(B)** was true for Han but not Roman civilization.

48. (B) A social hierarchy was common to all three and is also key to state formation.

49. (C) Monastic life refers to life in a monastery or, in this case, a nunnery. Monasticism represented one of the few exits for women from the generally restrictive gender roles of family life of the classical and postclassical worlds.

50. (D) Asoka moved the Maurya Empire toward Buddhism; Constantine's conversion moved Rome toward Christianity (and had more of a lasting impact in European civilization than Asoka's conversion did in India).

51. (D) Roman imperial rule depended on a combination of military occupation and local assistance.

52. (D) Nomads frequently served to communicate ideas and trends from one distant civilization to another. This helped to foster trade between civilizations.

53. (B) The proximity to older centers of civilization helped the Eastern Roman world during the breakdown of the Roman imperial unity.

54. (C) The Roman Empire formed a near complete rim around the Mediterranean, the richest region under Roman control.

55. (A) The "overexpansion" of the Roman Empire is a well-studied phenomenon and is intimately connected with dependence on unreliable hired mercenaries to represent Roman authority in far-flung regions.

56. (C) As indicated in question 53, this is a matter of factual knowledge that one needs to become familiar with.

57. (B) The concepts of citizenship (as opposed to subject status) or elected representation of nonaristocratic elements in government was underdeveloped to nonexistent in the civilizations listed other than the Roman civilization.

58. (D) Referring to question 44, choice **(D)** is most true even taking into consideration variations across city-states.

59. (C) Referring to question 11, the Old Testament of the Bible is derived from Jewish holy texts.

60. (D) The Ziggurats were massive monuments built during Sumerian and Mesopotamian times; Doric, Ionic, and Corinthian are all styles associated with columns, and the Parthenon is the most famous classical Greek structure to survive into the modern era.

61. (C) The Persian Empire was the largest empire in the ancient world until the days of Alexander, and it was the first to encompass land in Asia, Africa, and Europe. It was the European ambitions of Persian imperial power and also its time frame, 550 to 330 BCE, that made this empire a constant threat to Greek independence.

62. (A) The bullets form a useful reminder of key features of Indian geography—especially the mention of monsoon weather patterns!

63. (D) Tension between regional autonomy and central authority is an abiding theme in the history of the Indian subcontinent.

64. (B) The Hindu tradition and caste system are trademarks of early Indian culture, while the other choices contain a grain of truth at best.

65. (B) Buddhism, Christianity, Judaism, and Islam all trace their origins to the teachings of a central or founding figure. Hinduism stands apart with its absence of a prophetic founding figure; its central tenets were compiled over centuries and collected in holy texts such as the Vedas.

66. (D) Hinduism relies on texts, the Vedas being key, as a founding impulse, not the revelatory experiences of a prophetic or divine individual like the others listed in choices **(A)** through **(C)**.

67. (A) Rejection of caste is Buddhism's signal break with Hindu tradition.

68. (A) Dharma teaches acceptance of one's caste and role as key to spiritual peace and blessing.

69. (B) *The Analects* are a collection of Confucius's writings. Confucianism is not a spiritual faith but is closer to a political philosophy.

70. (C) The concept of zero is most associated with the Gupta Empire, a fact that one needs to become familiar with.

71. (D) Buddhists carried over the belief in reincarnation from Hinduism.

72. (C) Later empires to rule India, such as the Mughal (and even the British), confronted the same challenge. Recognizing long-term patterns like these are crucial for success in this advanced placement course.

73. (A) The classical period, lasting roughly from 1000 BCE to 600 CE, saw state and imperial structures grow to become quite refined and stable after millennia of evolution in the major centers of civilization. Stable imperial authority was the key to long-distance trade.

74. (D) Reviewing questions 67 and 71, Buddhism is viewed as a modification of Hinduism.

75. (B) Buddhism generally spread north and east but not much farther west than Persia or Central Asia, ruling out Buddhist presence in Mesopotamia.

76. (D) Reflective of the generally decentralized nature of the Hindu faith, castes have developed on an occupational and village-by-village basis, making thousands the best choice.

77. (A) The Koran is Arabic in origin while the Vedas and Bhagavad Gita have backgrounds from India.

78. (B) Choices **(C)** and **(D)** can be eliminated immediately. Looking at the remaining, China maintained generally superior craftsmanship and manufacturing capacity until the Industrial Revolution after the year 1800.

79. (B) The key cause to the rise of the world's population was the development of agriculture, which provided a reliable food supply that then in turn snowballed into other developments such as urbanization, job specialization, organized governments, and organized religion.

80. (A) The image shows language groups that developed from prehistorical Indo-Europeans who originated in Central Asia/South Russia and later spread from Western Europe to South Asia/India.

81. (D) Spanish developed from the Italic and Latin branches of Proto-Indo-European.

82. (C) The ancient Egyptians attributed the great benefits of the Nile River valley to divine blessing in the form of the River Nile, which was one deity in the pantheon of their polytheistic gods.

83. (A) Due to their role as great traders and the spreading of an alphabet to Greece and the larger Mediterranean world, the Phoenicians have often been called *carriers of civilizations.*

84. (B) The ancient world was afflicted by various plague outbreaks that spread around the world through trade routes and other forms of interaction.

85. (A) Christianity reached Ireland from the Roman province of Britain as early as the 300s CE through missionaries such as St. Patrick.

86. (A) The ruins of Mohenjo-Daro were a part of the Harappan or Indus River Valley civilization that disappeared around 1500 BCE.

87. (B) Archaeologists have determined that the Indus River/Harappan civilization at Mohenjo-Daro engaged in extensive urban planning that included indoor plumbing and a complex sanitation system that removed waste water from the city and tried to protect the city from floods.

88. (C) Filial piety, or devotion to earthly relations of obligation and submission, is a crucial tenet of Confucianism.

89. (A) By imposing a set of obligations for correct behavior upon the ruling elite, including emperors, it broke with previous systems that only bent the lower classes to their military and governing will.

90. (D) The Neolithic or Agricultural Revolution made it possible for larger populations to settle. The construction of megalithic architecture required organized governments. The primary purpose of Stonehenge is still not definitively known but probably has to do with the organization of religion around the worship of the sun.

91. (B) Writing developed from the need to record more than just simple economic transactions or kingship lineages. This shows a complex society that gave value to the written word.

92. (D) Writing was used to record formal agreements between individuals and groups.

93. (D) The Mandate of Heaven was adopted by the Zhou Dynasty to explain the changes in the dynastic cycle. This defining feature of traditional China justifies the replacement of an aging dynasty with a newer dynasty and gives divine approval.

94. (B) After the fall of the Han, no one dynasty would rule the traditional core of China until the emergence of the Sui dynasty in 581 CE. It is also the era when Buddhism made great headway in China.

95. (A) Ancient Greeks settled colonies as far away as the Black Sea, Iberia, and North Africa, which provided the homeland in Greece with necessary food grain supplies, markets for their trade goods, and contacts with other civilizations and peoples.

96. (D) Romans adopted writing from the Greek settlers in southern Italy, who had been influenced by the Phoenicians. The coin clearly shows writing along the left-hand side of the coin.

97. (B) The Sermon on the Mount reinforces the equality before God in Christianity and in many other faiths. Lines such as "Blessed are the meek: for they shall inherit the earth" and focus on loving one's neighbor and one's enemy promoted unity among believers.

98. (A) The Hammurabi Code of Law grew out of a harsh environment that emphasized revenge and inequality over social justice. Later law codes such as Rome's emphasized the state's monopoly on justice and violence.

99. (D) Beginning in the fourth century, Germanic invasions gradually weakened the Roman Empire and eventually toppled it when in 476 CE Germanic Visigoths overthrew the Roman Emperor.

100. (C) The caste system in India was thought to have developed from the Vedic culture of the Aryans, and the Laws of Manu were an early book from that tradition. The Vedic belief system later developed into Hinduism, which even today reinforces the caste system.

Chapter 2

101. (D) The Mongol expansion stopped in Eastern Europe, in what constitutes present-day Romania.

102. (D) Silk Roads passed through the Central Asian heartlands of the Mongol Empire.

103. (C) This merit system helped to explain the consistently superior quality of Mongol military forces. Nomadic people, not possessing property in land, are generally less inculcated with a respect for inherited wealth and lineage.

104. (C) The phalanx infantry formation was a Greek military technique where the soldiers aligned in a massive rectangular formation.

105. (B) Kiev was ravaged by the Mongols in late 1240. Kiev never recovered its preeminent status in Russian civilization.

106. (C) Mesopotamia in general, and Baghdad in particular, represented the economic and administrative heart of the Islamic world. Choices **(B)** and **(D)** occurred outside the time frame of Abbasid rule, and the Crusades never represented a mortal threat to Islamic civilization.

107. (A) Kublai Khan ruled from the imperial center at Beijing, though he had traditional Mongol-style tents (or yurts) placed in the Forbidden City just to show who was boss!

108. (C) Mongols were more appreciative of trade as a source of taxation, as well as new ideas from other civilizations, than were traditional Chinese elites.

109. (C) After the death of Genghis Khan the Mongol Empire was split into a number of khanates. These root-word games may seem trivial now but are important later on in the course, since across the globe nationhood winds up replacing all manner of monarchy and aristocratic rule. *Kingdom*, *principality*, *empire*, and *county* are of similar derivation.

110. (D) Known in the West as Tamerlane, Timur-I Lang's brief fourteenth-century expansion reached Persia, the Fertile Crescent, India, and southern Russia.

111. (D) Mongol contact with Chinese civilization made the Mongols a conduit for gunpowder to the West.

112. (A) Integration of west, central, eastern, and southern Africa into world trade was achieved via Muslim contact as well as trans-Saharan and Indian Ocean trade networks.

113. (D) Refer to the explanation in question 112. The Sahara Desert lies in the northern third of the African continent.

114. (C) State structures arise in part to reinforce class division, protect elites, and suppress slave uprisings. The archaeological, anthropological, and historical records do not show endemic class conflict to be a feature of stateless societies.

115. (C) Choice (**A**) is accurate for some but not all of postclassical black Africa. Choices (**B**) and (**D**) are not accurate descriptors of the same.

116. (A) Coptic Christianity's reach was limited roughly to Ethiopia. The other choices had little to no presence whatsoever.

117. (D) Muslim rule spread out of Arabia, across North Africa, and around the Strait of Gibraltar into the Iberian Peninsula in the seventh and eighth centuries CE. None of the other choices adjoin North Africa.

118. (C) Egypt's position at the northeast corner of the African continent near the isthmus of Suez has made it a crucial entry point into Africa since the dawn of civilization.

119. (C) The Bedouin, while many converted, are an Arabian ethnic group. The Berbers are a North African group exposed very early to Islam. The Ethiopians remained Christian, and the South African Khoisan and Zulu remained (more or less) unconverted to Islam.

120. (A) Coptic Christianity has been a mass faith in these societies from the days of the Roman Empire up until the present. Refer to question 116.

121. (D) Sudanic states spanned the Sahel band of grassland where the southern Sahara Desert transitions into the savanna and tropical climates of central Africa. Congo (sometimes spelled Kongo and called Zaire in the mid- to late twentieth century) is a central African society based around the Congo River, the second longest river in Africa.

122. (D) This is a popular question on world history exams. Levels of planning and organization required to carry out this trade rivaled those associated with early Atlantic crossings of Columbus and others.

123. (D) More commonly known as Mansa Musa; an easy mnemonic device (MMM) is used to associate him with the correct West African kingdom of the postclassical era—Mali (Mansa Musa from Mali).

124. (B) In the early postclassical era Western Europe (cities A, C, and D) was slowly regenerating centralized political authority and long-distance trade, while literacy and urbanization was just beginning to penetrate Russia (city E). In the same period, roughly 600 to 1000, West Africa was a center of all three.

125. (D) Take note that these three important West African kingdoms of the postclassical era have a chronological order that matches their alphabetical order.

126. (C) Devout Muslims did not practice ancestor worship but did relax female dress codes that were growing stricter in the rest of Islamic civilization at the time. This process of religious adaptation is an example of syncretism, or adjustment and combination of ideas.

127. (C) Swahili dates from the expansion of Islam into sub-Saharan Africa and is spoken across a vast expanse of territory. Arabic and Bantu are the two largest linguistic groups among the choices, with Yoruba and Berber being more localized tongues.

128. (B) The Swahili coast formed the western rim of the Indian Ocean trade network, where goods of the Middle East, South Asia, and East Asia were all available.

129. (C) Timbuktu is an important postclassical West African city. While some of the other choices may be a bit obscure, you should be sure that Timbuktu was NOT on the East African coast.

130. (D) Ivory is taken mainly from elephant tusks and has been worked by artisans from many civilizations—including African ones. The other listed materials are more associated with Mediterranean civilization (marble, oil paint, mosaic tile) or China (jade).

131. (B) In sub-Saharan Africa a higher proportion of elite individuals converted to Islam, perhaps due to closer contact with Muslim merchants, than did persons of lower social status.

132. (D) In no region listed did a majority convert to Islam, with the possible exception of Indonesia.

133. (D) Lack of a clear succession principle has been a lasting source of conflict in the religion and politics of Islamic civilization.

134. (C) Islamic civilization at its height encompassed more territory than the others listed. Keep in mind that Mongol power never penetrated Africa.

135. (A) The Bedouin people who populated the Arabian peninsula prior to the rise of Islam fall into the category of pastoral nomadic.

136. (D) Muhammad's retreat to Medina and his triumphant return to Mecca are seminal events in the early spread of the Islamic faith.

137. (C) Baghdad was the center of the Abbasid caliphate, and Istanbul became the capital of the Ottoman Empire.

138. (C) Khadija, daughter of Khuwaylid, was the wealthy widow of a prominent merchant.

139. (D) The other choices translate, roughly, as follows: *hijab*—clothing that preserves female modesty; *hajj*—pilgrimage to Mecca; *hadith*—the sayings and actions of Muhammad not contained in the Koran.

140. (C) These are the only two that shared space and time with the expanding Umayyad caliphate.

141. (A) The Indus River valley of northwest India had been a target of imperial conquest from the days of Alexander, and Spain and Morocco was the farthest westward outpost of the old Roman Mediterranean imperium. Islam at its height guided the trade and collected the knowledge of this vast, rich, and ancient zone of civilized humanity.

142. (D) *Dhimmi* translates roughly to "people of the book," which takes in the Abrahamic faiths and even Hinduism, but not animism, which was dismissed as paganism.

143. (C) Women were not allowed to have multiple spouses. The other choices form a decent summary of rights women had.

144. (B) In comparison with contemporary civilizations, women in the Islamic world experienced the greatest latitude in both the private and public spheres.

145. (C) The Umayyad caliphate (680–750) achieved the initial expansion of Islamic power in the decades and centuries after the death of Muhammad. The longer-lasting Abbasid caliphate (750–1258) oversaw a consolidation of Islamic power, continuing until it was toppled by Mongol invasions in the mid-thirteenth century.

146. (D) As a nice round number, you can keep in mind that in about the year 1000 CE Baghdad was perhaps the most sophisticated city on the planet. Only Chinese urban centers would have rivaled it.

147. (D) This serves as a useful summary of areas that flowered in what historians consider an Islamic golden age. Abbasid openness to conversion of non-Arabs to Islam (less true in the Umayyad period) fostered a period of vibrant cultural and intellectual exchange.

148. (D) Founding state religion of the Roman Empire did not survive the empire's decline as state religion while Islam survived the decline of the Abbasid caliphate and remained the dominant belief system in the Middle East even after the collapse of the caliphate. While in decline, the Abbasid rulers did not convert to a new religion.

149. (A) In more Eurocentric terms, Anatolia has been termed the "Near East," as distinct from the "Middle East" surrounding the Fertile Crescent or the "Far East" that generally refers to China and Japan.

150. (D) European military outposts lasted several centuries at most. Jerusalem has never been a Christian town, and Islam split into the Sunni and Shia branches in the seventh century (the Crusades were mainly a twelfth-century phenomenon).

151. (B) While complex sedentary social organization was emerging or established in all of the other choices, none of them rivaled Chinese or Islamic levels of sophistication.

152. (A) Mass conversion of South Asians to Islam would have to wait until the period of the Delhi Sultanate and the Mughal Empire, beginning in the thirteenth century. Anatolia, Egypt, and Morocco all saw considerable conversion rates. China never fell under Muslim control.

153. (D) Steam power is quintessentially modern and can be traced to eighteenth-century Great Britain. All postclassical civilizations qualify as premodern.

154. (D) The Slavic people were influenced by Byzantium. Take note that all of the regions listed in the question are Slavic regions.

155. (D) The eastern Mediterranean had been predominantly culturally Greek from the classical era and remained so until the arrival of the Ottoman Turks in the fifteenth century CE. The reversion from Latin back to Greek in both church and state affairs after the fall of the Western Roman Empire is evidence of this tendency.

156. (A) Neither Scandinavia, India, nor sub-Saharan Africa is adjacent to the choke point between the Black and Mediterranean seas that made Byzantium such a key trade hub in the ancient world.

157. (C) The Justinian code established a lasting legal framework, Byzantine bureaucracy is famously complex, and the Hagia Sophia was a monument to architectural grandeur. All date from the period of Justinian's rule. Diocletian launched a series of reforms that slowed, but did not reverse, the decline of the Western Roman Empire. Constantine is known for adopting Christianity as the state religion of the Roman Empire, Osman was the founding sultan of the Ottoman Empire.

158. (D) Byzantine power was influential abroad, as toward the north in Russia. However, military conquest and formal annexation of territory was not a Byzantine strong suit.

159. (B) Early Russian civilization is known as "Kievan Rus."

160. (C) Refer to question 105. Lasting from the 880s to the 1240s, Kievan Rus represents an early example of the slow trend toward centralization of political power and territorial expansion that characterized trends in European monarchy in later centuries.

161. (B) In a time of collapsed authority, banditry, and relative chaos following the failure of a Confucian state (the Han), Buddhism's orientation away from earthly troubles and toward a better hereafter attracted followers. Many of them lived on or near increasingly influential monasteries.

162. (C) This is a neat bit of dynastic trivia that will gain relevance again in twentieth and twenty-first century relations between the Chinese central government and the Tibet and Xinjiang regions that were first brought under Chinese rule during the Tang era.

163. (D) Prominent families, through test preparation of their children for civil service exams or bribery, tended to remain ensconced in positions of power in the Chinese bureaucracy; other choices may have been true in rare cases but do not rise to the level of being the "best" choice to answer this question.

164. (D) Punitive measures by Tang emperors, such as confiscation of monastic lands that had gone untaxed, reduced but did not eliminate Buddhist influence.

165. (B) Neo-Confucianism dates from the Song era and attempted to merge certain basic elements of Confucianism, Daoism, and Buddhism.

166. (D) Occupying the highest mountain plateau in the world, Tibetans have kept pretty much to themselves in world history; Jurchens, Turks, and Mongols are all central Asian nomadic groups.

167. (D) The Grand Canal connects the Yangtze and the Yellow river valleys, China's two most densely populated regions. Connecting the two was an important step forward in the process of Chinese unification.

168. (A) Arranged marriage and concubinage are also traditional and predate the Song era. Divorce rights and the one-child policy date from the communist era.

169. (D) China generated perhaps the largest share of key inventions of the premodern era. The rise of the Industrial Revolution in the West changed all that. Steam power dates from eighteenth-century England.

170. (D) Specifically, the Jinshi was a group composed of individuals who placed highest in the imperial examinations given every three years from the Sui dynasty of the early seventh century all the way down to 1905, when the examination system was abolished (with the exception only of a period during the Yuan dynasty when exams were suspended for a time).

171. (C) This choice is going to be incorrect about every Chinese society up until 1949, with the brief exception of the Taiping Rebellion of the 1860s.

172. (C) Areas of Japanese state formation and society listed in the other choices mirrored Chinese patterns more closely.

173. (D) Chinese naval capacity had not yet reached the level of sophistication to enable blue-water (distant from coastline) explorations necessary to meet Polynesian peoples in the Tang-Song era.

174. (B) Written in approximately 1008 CE, Lady Murasaki's *Tale of Genji* captures the pomp and circumstance of court life in the Heian era of Japanese history.

175. (C) The main trend in the postclassical era was for societies to move from a slave-based economic and social structure to one we call feudal. The similarities between European and Japanese feudalism stem in part from the relative isolation from global trade routes (as compared to the Byzantine or Islamic civilizations at the time) and the resultant necessity to base economic activity around cultivation of the land both civilizations shared.

176. (D) "High Middle Ages" refers to a period from about 1000 to 1300 and connotes something of a recovery from the Dark Ages that followed the fall of Rome in the fifth century. **(A)** predate the High Middle Ages, while **(B)** and **(C)** occurred after.

177. (D) Absorbed into the Muslim world, much of Spain did not experience a collapse in central authority to the same degree as the other regions listed.

178. (C) Even European ruling elites tended to be illiterate in the first centuries after the fall of Rome. Peasant illiteracy is not as surprising perhaps. Monasteries were outposts of reading and writing in this period.

179. (A) Ibn Battuta observes and is taken aback by the mixing of adult men and women who are not married to each other.

180. (C) The pyramids of the Meso-Americans were not used as palaces as they would have been impractical but were used solely for religious practices such as human sacrifices and offerings. The building of these structures was done by the Mayans as a form of taxation and religious observance that glorified the rule of the Mayan dynasties.

181. (D) The Incas developed quipu to keep records, although their exact use is still being investigated.

182. (D) The reading shows Early Russia having a positive view of Byzantine church architecture, rituals, music, and generosity. Russia later adopted many Byzantine cultural aspects.

183. (D) The Indian Ocean trade encompassed areas such as China, the Middle East, and East Africa but did not include trade directly with Europe because it was blocked by land. Later the Suez Canal would be built and direct trade between Europe and the Indian Ocean would be possible.

184. (A) The seasonal monsoon winds enabled movement across the Indian Ocean.

185. (D) In the early eighth century, Muslim warriors crossed the Straits of Gibraltar to begin the conquest of Visigoth Hispania in the Iberian Peninsula.

186. (B) The phrases such as "Beware of this world with all wariness" and rejecting worldly desires show Sufi asceticism and a less doctrinaire form of Islam.

187. (B) During the Abbasid dynasty the Islamic cities of Baghdad and Cordova were great centers of learning, especially scientific learning in astronomy, optics, and navigation.

188. (B) Many aspects of Chinese culture such as Buddhism, Confucianism, Daoism, and the writing system were introduced to Japan from the fourth to the eighth century.

189. (A) Buddhism, like Christianity, offers the option of a monastic lifestyle as a show of devotion.

190. (A) Europeans feared the Mongols as barbarian warriors similar to the Huns who contributed to the fall of the Roman Empire. Descriptions such as Paris's would have solidified this feeling.

191. (D) Marco Polo as a traveler with his father and uncle were accepted as merchants, and his long time in the East had given Marco a positive view of the Mongols as well as other peoples of the East.

192. (D) India was a great cultural influence on Southeast Asia, which can be seen in its religious traditions, architecture, dance, and writing system.

193. (A) Angkor Wat was originally a Hindu temple complex but was converted to and remains a Buddhist temple complex and monastery.

194. (A) The phrase "God, there is no god but he" and numerous references to "he" "Him" and "His" strongly show monotheism and rejects polytheism as the main belief of Islam.

195. (D) The image shows Persian or Turkish musicians on the back of a camel that inhabits the western (non-Han Chinese) areas that had long had contact and trade with peoples west of China.

196. (A) Arab and Persian scholars had built upon the achievements of the ancient Greeks in the areas of astronomy and navigation. Although invented in late antiquity in the Hellenistic age, Arabs and Persians further developed the astrolabe into one of the great achievements of the Islamic world.

197. (A) The Byzantines used the policy of caesaropapism, which combined both secular and religious power in the position of their emperors. The image shows the emperor being flanked by both soldiers and clerics.

198. (A) The Tang dynasty was a time of expanding trade. Complex economic practices would have been necessary for economic growth.

199. (B) Phrases such as "source of legitimacy for their rule," "gained recognition," and "political alliances" show how political considerations were important in the conversion to Islam. Conversion was of a top-down nature.

200. (A) The phrase in the early part of the excerpt "They did not . . . give up their religious . . . traditions" shows how Islam coexisted with previous belief systems.

Chapter 3

201. (D) European firearms were superior to African weapons and highly sought after by Africans themselves.

202. (C) Portuguese sailors were the first Europeans to venture down the West African coastline, starting in the early fifteenth century. They were in the best position to set up slave-trading posts (called factories) after the discovery of the New World. The shift to plantation agriculture there sent demands for slave labor skyrocketing.

203. (D) Roughly speaking, the sixteenth century was spent plundering the New World while the seventeenth was spent carving plantations out of the wilderness. The plantation economy was booming in the eighteenth century, and by the nineteenth century industrialization and wage labor was the most profitable investment for capital.

204. (B) Coastal kingdoms participated in what historians term a "gun and slave cycle," in which they traded individuals captured inland for guns and then employed those weapons in the capture of more people, pressing farther and farther inland.

205. (D) Northeast Africa is much closer to the Arab and Indian zones of the world economy than the Atlantic world. As for the other choices, ivory, gold, and domestic slaves were in demand around the Indian Ocean basin, and this trade was carried out by Muslim merchants who would have been the buyers of imported copies of the Koran.

206. (C) These Dutchmen came to be known as Boers (Dutch for "farmers"). Their descendants have been in South Africa for longer than most persons of European descent living in North America can claim to have been living here.

207. (C) These conflicts at first caused migrations of Boers away from coastal areas to the interior (the "Great Trek") and later bubbled over into the Boer War circa 1900.

208. (B) The estimated mortality rate was 30 percent on African soil and 10 percent at sea. Tales, poems, and paintings of sharks following slave ships across the oceans serve as a constant reminder of the horrors of dead or dying people being thrown overboard.

209. (D) Sugar cultivation on the Caribbean Islands, including Haiti, Jamaica, and Barbados, involved notoriously high mortality rates. No significant slave trade to Argentina ever developed. The tobacco, rice, and later, cotton that were cultivated in the temperate climate of the southern thirteen colonies allowed for a natural increase of the population of enslaved Africans. This is one reason why the black population of the United States continued to grow even after the Atlantic slave trade was outlawed in 1808. In fact, an internal slave trade from the older tidewater plantation areas of Maryland and Virginia down to the expanding cotton belt across Georgia, Alabama, Mississippi, Louisiana, and Texas developed after 1808.

210. (B) Slavery lasted in Brazil until 1888; it was declared illegal in Mexico in 1810, in Haiti in 1804, in the United States in 1865, and in Cuba in 1886.

211. (B) While the sugar plantations of the Caribbean Island, taken together, made up the main destination of enslaved Africans, the sugar plantations of Brazil's Atlantic coast attracted more slave ships than any other single colony on its own. The British thirteen colonies were never a major destination in the slave trade compared with points farther south.

212. (B) England was the first of these choices to ban slave trade. This began in 1808.

213. (A) The Atlantic slave trade grew during the Enlightenment era and flew in the face of concepts of natural rights belonging to all humans.

214. (C) While Russian monarchy was the largest contiguous land empire in history, one must keep in mind that much of it was relatively empty Siberian land.

215. (D) Referring to the previous question, the lands to the east of the Ural Mountains that were gained were vast and sparsely populated.

216. (D) Remember that St. Petersburg (Peter's town) is to the *west* of Moscow, a reminder of Peter the Great's general policy course.

217. (A) Serfdom was so woven into the fabric of Russian life that it was applied to the new factory system when it arrived.

218. (C) Monarchs, in general, were searching for paths to increased royal authority in the period after 1450. For Russia, westernization would serve that purpose.

219. (A) Russian eastward ambition stretched through Siberia, across the Bering Strait, and into Alaska. The United States approved the purchase of Alaska from the Russians in 1867. This event is often referred to as Seward's folly or Seward's icebox.

220. (D) Regarding world trade, Russia played to its own strengths, supplying resources that its vast territory could produce in bulk.

221. (D) Russian expansion has tended to be land based and not naval throughout the course of its history.

222. (A) No European monarch with a sense of pride wanted to fall too far behind in military capacity. We can rule out choice **(D)** if we refer to question 221.

223. (C) The early settlers of Massachusetts, the Puritans, were British citizens seeking greater religious freedom. We have no similar phenomenon in the settlement of Spanish Latin America, perhaps because religious minorities were effectively eliminated in a series of campaigns in Spain spanning from the Reconquista of 1492 when Jews and Muslims were expelled from Spain into the period of the Inquisition of the sixteenth and seventeenth centuries where Catholic orthodoxy was imposed by force on the population.

224. (C) This was particularly true in British North America.

225. (A) Terms like "mestizo" or "mulatto" arose in Spanish Latin America to reflect the commonplace racial mixing that took place there. Skin color affected social status in both locations, however.

226. (B) This can be explained in large part by the near complete disappearance of the indigenous population of the New World in the face of smallpox and war.

227. (C) These estates were called *encomiendas* and were crucial to the establishment of an agricultural economy in the Spanish New World. "Bourbon reforms" were enacted to tighten royal control as the *encomiendas* began to form power bases to challenge the rule of the Spanish monarchy in the seventeenth and eighteenth centuries.

228. (C) Columbus landed on Hispanola (which today contains the nations of Haiti and the Dominican Republic), abducted several indigenous Arawak/Carib native individuals, and returned to Spain. On subsequent voyages to the Caribbean, he set about the business of enslaving indigenous populations and setting them to work searching for gold.

229. (D) The choices above serve as a useful list to help remind us of the nuts and bolts of the move from "plunder to plantation."

230. (C) By the time sugar had supplanted silver as the New World's most valuable product, the Spanish monarchy had been displaced from key sugar-producing locations (the islands of Saint-Domingue, Jamaica, and Barbados being cases in point).

231. (A) The rise of northern European mercantile and naval interests in the seventeenth century make statements II and III inaccurate.

232. (D) Sugar, as in the Caribbean, was the initial generator of income in Brazil. Gold became important after its discovery in the Minas Gerais region.

233. (B) Peninsulares were people born in Spain. Creoles were Spaniards born in the New World. Mestizos were a mix of Spanish and Native American.

234. (C) Absolute monarchies would develop by 1750. They were not yet in place in 1450.

235. (B) The Italian Renaissance is credited with creating a transition from Medieval times to the making of early modern Europe. It was mainly a movement that found its expression through the arts, making it more of a cultural change than any of the other choices.

236. (C) Families such as the de' Medici (House of Medici) symbolize this phenomenon.

237. (D) The Spanish monarchy, like all monarchs of the late fifteenth century, was Catholic and sought religious uniformity throughout its kingdom. Be aware that the Huguenots were French Protestants who had yet to exist.

238. (D) In the years 1450 to 1750 the Western societies would process this knowledge to insert themselves as intermediaries in a new web of global trade.

239. (D) This seaward orientation makes it unsurprising that Portuguese mariners took a leading role in oceanic exploration after 1450.

240. (C) This shift in sea supremacy is best represented by the defeat of the Spanish Armada off the coast of England in 1588.

241. (D) Luther's orientation toward biblical, as opposed to Catholic, authority makes his rejection of this element of Christian faith implausible.

242. (D) Remember that he nailed his 95 Theses to a church door in Wittenberg, with the "W" pronounced as a "V," common to the German language.

243. (C) Jesuits were key to Catholic efforts to aggressively spread their brand of Christianity worldwide to counter the rise of new Protestant competitors.

244. (B) While the European population increased overall, growing commercialization of agriculture and enclosure movements that pushed peasants off the land swelled the ranks of proletarians (those who own nothing but their labor power).

245. (B) With time, scientific thinking began to displace religious thinking among educated elites in the West.

246. (C) The Enlightenment in many respects was a logical outgrowth of the Scientific Revolution; as the Scientific Revolution cast doubt on the rule of the church in the realm of ideas, the Enlightenment cast doubt on the rule of kings in the realm of human society.

247. (D) Nicolaus Copernicus was a Polish astronomer whose work disproved the earth as the center of the universe. These findings were later confirmed by Galileo's observations.

248. (C) The Englishman Isaac Newton can be viewed as the father of modern physics. His understanding of motion and gravity held sway until the work of Albert Einstein emerged in the early twentieth century.

249. (A) Locke's formulation of "natural rights" is a key Enlightenment concept.

250. (B) Other civilizations, as a rule, placed greater stock in religion, this being least true of the Chinese.

251. (D) Absolute monarchs, grown more rich and powerful through command of maritime trade and New World colonies, tended to centralize authority at the expense of the lesser aristocracy. The case of French monarchy and Louis XIV is a prime example.

252. (D) England stands apart from a trend toward absolute monarchy; patterns of limited monarchy dating back to the rise of Parliament in the twelfth century, and the Magna Carta of the thirteenth century, laid a basis for the emergence of a constitutional and not absolute monarchy in England.

253. (D) Parliament gained power to approve taxation and expenditure, also known as the "power of the purse," during the Glorious Revolution of 1689.

254. (C) Adam Smith was the foremost spokesman for the interests of a rising British merchant class seeking minimum interference from royal authority in business dealings.

255. (B) Divine right was a religious reflection of the rise of absolute monarchy; remember absolute monarchy and Enlightenment philosophy as being in opposition.

256. (D) In this arrangement peasants took raw material, often wool, into their cottages and performed labor there to contribute to the production of a finished manufactured product.

257. (C) Of the groups listed in the choices, proletarians had the fewest alternatives to factory work.

258. (D) Henry VIII famously split from the Catholic church and set up the Anglican church in order to pursue a divorce prohibited by Catholic regulations.

259. (D) These patterns are each repeated and amplified as Western maritime empires move to the center of the world economy in the period 1450–1750, integrating the New World into the Old.

260. (C) Awareness of this circumstance is key to understanding the move of the West toward the core of a new global economy in the period 1450–1750.

261. (D) Multiple factors came into play for this most important "nondecision" in world history.

262. (C) These islands off the coast of West Africa were suited for intensive sugar cultivation and were within easy reach of mariners who had yet to cross the Atlantic. Plantations were established in the first half of the fifteenth century by the Portuguese, and that language is still spoken on those islands today.

263. (D) Central America, home of the Aztecs, was "integrated" into the world economy after the arrival of Cortez in 1519.

264. (C) The Maori people are believed to have arrived in New Zealand sometime before the year 1300.

265. (D) The line, established in 1493 in a treaty signed in the city of Tordesillas in the Valladoid province of Spain, passes through South America in a manner that roughly divides the present-day nation of Brazil from the Spanish-speaking portions of the continent. Even today, Portuguese is the official language in Brazil.

266. (D) Dutch Java became a prototype for European colonization of non-American lands.

267. (D) Magellan himself never made it around the globe, but two of his ships did. He died in the Philippines in 1521.

268. (D) All of the choices are specific contributing factors to the important "power vacuum" that existed circa 1450.

269. (D) While choices **(A)**, **(B)**, and **(C)** look tempting, syphilis is a sexually transmitted disease that was introduced to the Europeans upon their arrival to the New World.

270. (A) The Columbian Exchange dramatically increased contact between societies in the Eastern and Western hemispheres. This included diseases, livestock, and crops.

271. (D) In every other body of water listed, the West encountered existing naval and coastal military presences that required sustained campaigns to overcome or with whom Western ships had to coexist.

272. (D) Sugar, tobacco, and coffee all had addictive properties, allowing for these commodities to be very profitable.

273. (C) The Congolese King Afonso's appeals to the Portuguese for the cessation of the slave trade in his territory were rebuffed. Middle Eastern, South Asian, and particularly East Asian civilizations were in a strong position to dictate terms of trade with the West in the period 1450–1750.

274. (D) Being the first to round the Cape of Good Hope and reach the Indian Ocean with the voyages of Vasco da Gama in 1495, the Portuguese followed up by seizing strategic positions at shipping choke points around the Indian Ocean basin soon thereafter.

275. (C) Dutch control of spice production in Java was a huge accomplishment for the Dutch.

276. (D) The shift from the Ming to the Qing is also important because the Ming were the last dynasty to effectively control interaction with the foreign world, particularly the West, and maintain terms advantageous to ruling Chinese elites.

277. (B) Mongol expansion touched major civilizations across the Eurasian landmass, and its collapse opened space for the emergence of new powers, particularly in the Muslim world. Additionally, new Russian and Chinese ruling dynasties emerged in the period following Mongol rule.

278. (C) Safavid Persia has become Iran and is still the center of the Shia branch of Islam today.

279. (B) The fifteenth century saw an expansion of Europe to the Americas, Africa, and Asia. Merchants and missionaries used maritime trade winds to facilitate their travels to these parts of the world.

280. (C) The monsoons are seen as both a blessing and a curse since they enable agriculture to flourish yet also bring flooding.

281. (A) Casta paintings reflect the rigid social class system that developed in the Spanish colonial Americas.

282. (D) The division of the region's people into economic classes was adopted from Europe, but the addition of racial divisions was new and unique in world history.

283. (D) The European conquest of port cities in South and Southeast Asia, combined with low-grade civil war associated with feudal conflicts, encouraged Japanese rulers of the Shogunate to be very wary of Christian missionaries and European traders.

284. (A) Coming out of the centuries of Mongol expansion and before when steppe nomads were viewed as the greatest threat, the Chinese of the early modern era did not view Europeans as more than an annoyance or minor threat.

285. (A) Gunpowder weaponry and technology gave these states the military edge over their opposition.

286. (C) The Muslim Mughals, being in a minority, generally practiced toleration toward their Hindu subjects and cooperated with local Hindu Rajput rulers.

287. (C) Hinduism's popularity was based on its long existence, flexibility, appropriation of other faiths, and state support. Islam, while emphasizing charity, does not impose abolition of class or gender hierarchies.

288. (D) Islamic calligraphy and minarets are well-known examples of Islamic design, and their presence indicate not a sharing of space between religions in this temple but a replacement.

289. (B) Christianity was seen as too different or counterintuitive to Chinese culture by scholars.

290. (C) Scholars and government officials were schooled and tested in Confucian classics, which looked down on other belief systems.

291. (A) Kings and their states with increasing taxation had the financial backing for supporting authors, artists, craftsman, and explorers as well as scientists, all of whom increased the prestige and glory of the monarchs.

292. (D) Despite great cultural flowerings in both China and the Islamic Middle East, an orthodoxy had set in these societies and discouraged intellectual pursuits, which were seen as of little value. The ending of the voyages of the Chinese explorer Zheng He is a famous example.

293. (B) The trade in African slaves, European manufactured goods, and American crops dominated the trade relations in the Atlantic world in the Early Modern Era.

294. (A) European nation-states' trade operated with mercantilist laws in order to increase their nation's wealth in relation to other nation-states.

295. (D) Medieval and early modern European rulers, like rulers long before, them had a symbiotic relationship with religion and established belief systems.

296. (A) Johann Gutenberg's printing press spread Luther's ideas far and wide, and any attempt against him would have made him a martyr and maybe spread his ideas even further.

297. (B) Rice agriculture requires an initial planting of the rice plants close together and then for them to be replanted with more space. This intensive labor plus the constant monitoring of the water level and the creation of terraces makes rice agriculture one of the most labor-intensive types of farming.

298. (A) Chinese influence had been in Vietnam since the second century CE and is shown in the longstanding respect for Confucian values, Chinese writing, architecture, and the emperor system.

299. (A) The scholar class in both China and Korea were education in Confucian classics and ethics. They therefore felt threatened by Buddhism, which challenged filial piety and other aspects of Confucianism. In particular the author identifies the monastic practice of separating the sexes as damaging to Korean tradition.

300. (C) Traditional Chinese society, like most societies, was male dominated or patriarchal.

Chapter 4

301. (D) When you hear or see the word *industrial*, think of the word *factory*. All of the other choices were preindustrial motives as well.

302. (C) "Divide and conquer" remained a key tactic of control for colonial powers since the Dutch pioneered it in seventeenth-century Java.

303. (D) These "men on the spot" had considerable latitude in the relations they established with indigenous elites as they penetrated the subcontinent. Preindustrial communication delays meant reports to and instructions from England were many months in transit.

304. (D) The role of the colony in the industrial era is not to be a center of industrial production.

305. (B) Colonial society functioned best when each person knew his or her "place." Traditional hierarchical structures assisted in this arrangement.

306. (A) Colonialists were influenced in many ways by the culture of the "native," but they drew the line at religion in general.

307. (B) Loyal cooperation was more valued than coerced obedience when it came to managers who were often trusted with important administrative tasks.

308. (D) The famine in Bengal flies in the face of claims by British imperialists that their rule banished famine in India.

309. (B) Ritual wife burning was targeted by British colonial officials as a barbaric practice that must be brought to a stop.

310. (D) China and Brazil were not industrial rivals; in fact, the only non-Western nation to gain this status by 1900 was Japan.

311. (D) Major direct military clashes between rival imperialists exploded in the First World War, not before.

312. (B) Independent but influenced by the West were important commonalities of all of these regions.

313. (B) No white minority of any significant size (relative to total population) has ever settled in India.

314. (D) All of the choices capture the mix of divide and conquer, paternalism, and racism that characterized the colonial relationship.

315. (B) Particularly racist notions about the African inability to learn, notoriously prevalent in Belgian rule of the Congo for instance, meant that colonial administrations viewed setting up anything more than rudimentary schooling as a waste of time and resources. Church groups did it out of charity if any Westerners bothered to set up schools at all.

316. (D) Again, the colony was not a place to be industrialized but rather a place that might supply the raw material and might purchase the product.

317. (D) Famously, no Africans were involved in negotiations that, to a large degree, drew political boundaries that remain in place on the continent today.

318. (C) Gandhi was radicalized by racist prohibitions in South Africa that barred him from freely practicing the profession he had studied in London, law.

319. (D) With the revolution starting in Great Britain, it makes sense that it would spread to continental Europe and then the United States.

320. (B) Slavery is exceedingly undemocratic—contrary to the democracy that was being fought for.

321. (A) Looking over the events, we see that the formation of the National Assembly must come first and that the rule of Napoleon must come last.

322. (D) *Declaration of the Rights of Man and Citizen* contained key rights that included liberty, property, security, and resistance to oppression.

323. (D) As the leading element of the Third Estate before the revolution, this group enjoyed a high status after the revolution, an unsurprising outcome.

324. (B) Family ties with the deposed French monarchy and fear of the spread of revolution on the part of neighboring monarchies made imitation or indifference toward the events in France impossible.

325. (C) Records are incomplete but estimates range from 16,000 to 40,000; these numbers pale in comparison with twentieth-century instances of political violence.

326. (D) Sexist practices proved very durable and were codified in the Napoleonic Code.

327. (B) Classical liberal ideas are most closely associated with the interests of the rising middle class and bourgeoisie of nineteenth-century Europe.

328. (A) Conservatives sought to preserve aristocratic privilege as much as possible while radicals sought to improve the status of working people. Refer to question 327.

329. (D) Russian czarism was the strongest monarchy in Europe and successfully insulated its society from Western political trends following Russia's defeat of Napoleon's invasion in 1812.

330. (C) The 1830s saw the Reform Bill in England and Jacksonian democracy in the United States, where voting rights were expanded to new segments of the population.

331. (D) Absolute monarchy can only be said to have existed in Russia, and it was on the defensive even there.

332. (D) Minimum-wage laws were not established until the New Deal era reforms of the 1930s.

333. (D) Locke was a late-seventeenth-century thinker, while the others would make their mark later in history.

334. (D) The U.S. Civil War, a massive resource base, nearly unrestricted immigration, and territorial expansion to the western portion of the North American continent all combined to make the United States a leading industrial power.

335. (A) The United States held on to slavery within its national borders until the Civil War of the 1860s.

336. (C) In particular, the rise of German naval capacity was seen as a threat by the British. It wouldn't be much longer before Germany was involved in two wars.

337. (C) Initial industrialization is often of the "light industrial" variety, focused around textile production. This is greatly different from what industrialization was to become.

338. (C) Business interests associated with liberal politicians generally opposed choices **(A)**, **(B)**, and **(D)**, but radical politicians demanded such reforms. Neither group would have supported a return of monarchy.

339. (A) The thirteen colonies cannot be said to have contained a "peasantry" on anything like the feudal terms that existed in France, while statements I and II were true for both.

340. (C) Workers did not organize what we recognize as unions until after they were brought together into factories and mines by the hundreds and thousands at a time.

341. (D) To oversimplify, Spencer can be viewed perhaps as combining the conclusions of Hobbes (life is "a war of each against all") and Darwin (natural selection) to come to the conclusion that "survival of the fittest" was the proper state for human affairs.

342. (B) Only Latin American nations fit this description.

343. (B) Latin American nations serve as something of a preview of the challenges of postcolonial development the rest of the developing world would face in the post–World War II era. Economic dependency on the West was chief among those challenges.

344. (D) Creole elites aimed for little more change than ejection of the peninsulares; Haiti's revolution showed the risks of slave uprisings for the Creole elites.

345. (D) Conscious of the rhetoric of the French Revolution, enslaved Haitians rose in revolt and achieved independence in 1803.

346. (C) This temporary decapitation of the Spanish Empire opened a window of opportunity for Creole self-government that sparked desires for complete independence.

347. (B) Portugal's king relocated to Brazil and declared it an independent monarchy in 1822. Every other Latin American colony became a republic.

348. (D) For large groups, then, the changes brought by independence were cosmetic, not profound.

349. **(C)** The year 1800 is a good, round year to imagine the Industrial Revolution gaining real momentum. Patterns of urbanization, factory work, and other items that we recognize to be "industrial" became increasingly prominent after that date.

350. **(C)** These men were known as *caudillos*, and their interference in politics has become such a pattern that historians speak of a "*caudillo* phenomenon" in Latin American history.

351. **(D)** In Latin American politics, Centralists tended to be liberal reformers with more ambitious modernization schemes while Federalists tended to be more conservative regional leaders looking to maintain the status quo.

352. **(B)** Descendants of the Creole elites continued to dominate politics no matter what political party happened to be in power.

353. **(C)** While the United States proclaimed a Monroe Doctrine opposing any possible "recolonization" of independent Latin American nations, it was the British navy that was the guarantor of security of any form in the Atlantic world of the first half of the nineteenth century.

354. **(C)** Local manufacturing for internal Latin American markets was difficult to get off the ground because low tariffs made it hard for infant industry to compete with cheaper goods manufactured in Great Britain or elsewhere.

355. **(D)** By the nineteenth century primary products of industrial production and food-stuffs to feed burgeoning populations in Europe and North America generated the bulk of Latin America's trade relations with the world.

356. **(A)** The Mexican-American War of the 1840s was a major victory for the United States in that it was able to conquer New Mexico, parts of northern Mexico, and California.

357. **(A)** This most closely matches a classic liberal political program and describes the Juarez regime that ruled in the mid-nineteenth century.

358. **(A)** The Mapuche and Auracanian people maintained armed resistance against white incursion into the late nineteenth century.

359. **(D)** Southern Europeans, Italians in particular, were attracted to Argentina in the decades before and after the turn of the twentieth century—a period of massive emigration to the United States as well. Inexpensive steam ship passage was key.

360. **(A)** Business interests and modernization have trumped liberal politics many times over in postcolonial societies.

361. **(D)** Spain's last remaining colonies were lost to the United States in this 1898 conflict.

362. **(D)** This episode dates from 1903 and occurred under the supervision of U.S. President Theodore Roosevelt.

363. (D) Mesoamerica was the most densely populated region of the New World when Cortez arrived there, and it became Spain's richest colony thanks to the labor of the millions of indigenous people who survived initial disease outbreaks. This dense indigenous population continued to be a force throughout Mexican history as witnessed by the emergence of prominent leaders of indigenous background such as Miguel Hidalgo and Benito Juarez.

364. (C) Yet, by 1914 neither would be formally colonized but both would be reduced to economically dependent relationships with the West.

365. (C) Turkey now occupies the Anatolian peninsula that was the heartland of the Ottoman Empire.

366. (D) This question serves as a useful listing of the Tanzimat reforms.

367. (C) Muhammad Ali's Egypt stands as a case of thwarted industrialization outside the West, contrasting with successful industrialization in Japan and Russia.

368. (D) This waterway was a hugely important shortcut around the African landmass.

369. (D) This trend tends to breed resentment and poverty in the countryside, which can build to unsustainable levels and explode into revolt.

370. (B) China enjoyed a favorable balance of trade during the Qing era all the way up until the advent of the opium trade in the early nineteenth century.

371. (D) Communism would have to wait until the twentieth century to become influential in China.

372. (C) This imperial arrogance causes a stunning lack of awareness of the danger the West would pose.

373. (B) Even in 1800, Chinese industrial capacity surpassed that of the British. For centuries the only commodity the British and other Westerners had that the Chinese desired was silver.

374. (A) In these respects the communist movement that emerged in the 1920s can be seen to be picking up where the Taiping movement of the 1850s and 1860s left off. Ideology was the difference, with the Taiping leaders being gripped by a sinified Christianity while the communist leaders were adhered to a sinified Marxism. Even here similarity persists since both ideologies were Western in origin.

375. (D) The Italians came relatively late to the nineteenth-century race for colonies and limited their ambitions to the African continent.

376. (C) The Tanzimat reforms were an Ottoman Empire initiative while the other four were Chinese movements.

377. (C) China's agricultural and urban heartlands lie roughly in the eastern coastal region between the Yellow and Yangtze rivers.

378. (A) Lin Zexu was an important nineteenth-century Chinese figure; this short primary document that he wrote is worth familiarizing yourself with.

379. (A) Inequality among the different social classes in France is considered to be one of the main causes leading to the Revolution in 1789.

380. (C) Within the Third Estate (bourgeoisie, peasants, and urban poor), only the bourgeoisie's condition was improved by the French Revolution and Napoleonic reforms.

381. (D) Many French soldiers were demoralized by both the conditions of fighting in Haiti with its high death toll due to disease plus the contradiction of their goals in Haiti with Republican ideals that they had been raised on.

382. (D) The British antislavery movement was just beginning in the 1780s and had not had much influence beyond England and the newly freed American colonies.

383. (B) The Tanzimat Reforms from the 1830s to 1870s removed the legal inequality against Christians and Jews and other minorities. These were part of modernization efforts after Ottoman losses in the Crimean War.

384. (A) Subject peoples such as Slavs and Arabs demanded more autonomy and even independence. This was part of a global process of rising nationalism in the nineteenth century.

385. (B) The closure of Japan came to an abrupt end soon after Perry's visit in 1853 and would soon provide an impetus for the modernizing reforms under the emperor Meiji.

386. (A) Japan's changes in the Meiji era are often compared to the lack of reforms in China during the same period. The 100 Days of Reform are a point in fact.

387. (D) Historians now discount the idea of Japanese modernization as a direct result of the arrival of the Americans. Many of the precursors of modernization were already in place in Tokugawa Japan.

388. (A) The unemployment created by the invention of labor-saving machines led some workers to take out their frustrations on the machines and those who owned them.

389. (C) Karl Marx saw history as a constant struggle between the "haves and have nots." He predicted that workers would overthrow the bourgeoisie and create a worker-run state.

390. (B) The mid-to late-nineteenth century saw a weakened China that was unable to control its own sovereignty. This period is part of what some Chinese call the "Century of Humiliations."

391. (A) The continent of Africa was divided up before, during, and after the Berlin Conference 1884–1885 in what was called the "Scramble for Africa."

392. (A) The introduction of New World crops such as corn and potatoes led to more food being produced with the intensification of farming.

393. (B) The Enlightenment was an intellectual movement in Europe during the late seventeenth and eighteenth centuries emphasizing reason and knowledge rather than religion and tradition. The printing of the *Encyclopedia* was an attempt to catalog and build upon all existing knowledge that could facilitate human progress.

394. (A) The Scientific Revolution led to the Industrial Revolution by the practical application of science in technology.

395. (D) Scholars agree that the Industrial Revolution began in Britain and Europe rather than in other areas of the world. However, historians are still debating why it began there.

396. (C) Britain had the right geography, government support, and infrastructure to encourage industrialization. It also had the right social conditions in a middle class that sought opportunities in industrialization.

397. (A) Many clergy in the Catholic Church refused to take the oath in the Civil Constitution of the Clergy, which the Pope had spoken out against and many felt would have subordinated the church to the new state.

398. (A) Hilaire Beloc was a historian writing from a Catholic perspective. His bias shows forth in his very negative descriptions of the French Revolution's actions toward the church, which he sees as "persecution," "cruelty," and a "failure."

399. (C) Thomas Malthus warned of the dangers of overpopulation due to the ability of the world's population to always exceed its ability to produce sufficient food. The only ways to keep the population in check were famines, diseases, and war.

400. (B) The Irish Potato Famine seems to demonstrate an instance where a population is not able to be sustained by the food production. In fact, Malthus predicted that Ireland would suffer "a check" on its population.

Chapter 5

401. (B) By the 1960s Western elites and general populations both accepted decolonization as something of an inevitability; France stands as something of an exception, fighting two bitter wars to maintain colonial holdings, one in Indonesia and the other in Algeria. Statement III is nonetheless mainly false.

402. (B) Liberal democracy fell in Russia, Germany, Italy, and across Eastern Europe in the period between the world wars, appearing to be a failed political arrangement to many. Its resurgence after World War II was reinforced by the emergence of the United States as a superpower.

403. (C) For starters, unlike all the other major combatants, United States factories were never successfully targeted for destruction and so the country emerged from the war with an unparalleled industrial capacity. Add to this the international influence of the U.S. military and cultural (Hollywood) presence and broad outlines of American power can be discerned.

404. (B) The United States committed itself to nuclear retaliation if Cold War allies faced Soviet military assault. Many historians credit this willingness to fight with never needing to—the principle of deterrence.

405. (D) These Cold War–era military alliances faced each other across a dividing line that Winston Churchill famously termed the Iron Curtain. For many decades World War III was expected to be fought between these two alliances.

406. (A) These actions are known to historians as de-Stalinization.

407. (D) Josip Tito's Yugoslavia mounted a more or less independent resistance to Nazi invasion during World War II, liberated itself from fascist occupation, and emerged as an independent socialist state after World War II.

408. (C) Certainly untrue, Soviet Cold War industry was the productive base for one side of the greatest arms race in history.

409. (D) The famous Marshall Plan, named after George Marshall, was an important factor in maintaining Western Europe as part of the liberal democratic and not socialist camp during the early phases of the Cold War.

410. (C) From June 1948 to May 1949 the Royal Air Force and United States Air Force organized flights to provide necessities to the people of West Berlin.

411. (D) Japanese workers are unionized but generally do not strike. They traditionally enjoy lifetime employment at a single firm in a broad social agreement that more or less has maintained labor peace.

412. (B) The two major wars occurred in Korea (1950–1953) and Vietnam (1955–1975), countries located in Asia.

413. (A) Choices I and II are true for both countries. Choice III is true for Korea and false for Vietnam.

414. **(C)** General Douglas MacArthur famously proposed using tactical nuclear weapons to turn the tide against Chinese communist forces that joined the battle in the Korean War. No prominent U.S. military or civilian official suggested dropping nuclear bombs on Vietnam, in public at least. Refer to question 413 as well.

415. **(D)** This campaign coincided with drought and crop failures that led to widespread food shortages.

416. **(D)** To wit, the famous "one-child" policy for urban families.

417. **(C)** Significant institutional and economic disruption resulted from this campaign that was both launched and dismantled by Mao.

418. **(D)** It's fair to say that the Chinese Communist Party has put striving for egalitarianism on the proverbial back burner for the time being.

419. **(A)** Since Deng Xiaoping became leader of the Chinese Communist Party in 1979, China has seen economic but not political reform.

420. **(B)** This is the defining challenge of postcolonial life.

421. **(D)** Not that there is a demonstrable connection between the two, if it is to be accepted at all that women's status is improving

422. **(A)** Patterns of underdevelopment, such as overspecialization in export of a few raw materials or crops set in motion in the colonial era, made achieving such ambitious economic goals a tall order for nationalist leaders.

423. **(B)** Most developing nations have experienced military rule at some point.

424. **(D)** Kwame Nkrumah was the leader of the first African nation to gain independence, Ghana, in 1957. The old colonial name used by the British, the Gold Coast, was replaced by Ghana as a reminder of ancient patterns of civilization that predated European colonization.

425. **(D)** Egypt, like the rest of Africa, still imports most of its durable consumer goods.

426. **(D)** Caste remains a defining feature of Indian civilization despite decades of (perhaps half-hearted) government efforts to reform it out of existence.

427. **(C)** The mere fact that the West did not have an influence makes the Iranian Revolution unique in twentieth-century history.

428. **(D)** Pakistan lost East Pakistan in 1972, which seceded and became the independent nation of Bangladesh.

429. **(C)** The Organization of Petroleum Exporting Countries (OPEC) fixes oil prices at levels agreed on by the governments of developing countries, not Western consumers.

430. (C) The Nationalist Party that negotiated independence in 1960 ruled an apartheid state where the majority black population could not vote.

431. (B) Steven Biko was an antiapartheid activist in the 1960s and 1970s who was killed while in police custody, while Mandela's involvement can be traced as far back as the 1950s and is forever identified with the twenty-six years he spent in prison while the antiapartheid struggle was carried on by his compatriots outside.

432. (D) Nigeria's petroleum industry is the main force behind its GDP.

433. (B) Be careful not to be too quick to pick choice **(A)**. European elites, particularly Central and Eastern European elites, were traumatized by the Bolshevik seizure of power in Russia, and the first promise of fascist regimes wherever they came to power was to stamp out the communist threat.

434. (C) "Il Duce" was invited to power by the king of Italy after the 1922 "March on Rome."

435. (C) Dating from 1910, the Mexican Revolution predates the next successful revolution of the twentieth century, the Bolshevik Revolution of 1917. The Chinese (1949) and Iranian (1979) revolutions occurred midcentury and after.

436. (C) The leading role played by mestizo and Indian elements in Mexican politics dates back to the prominence of Miguel de Hidalgo in the 1830s and continued through the era of Benito Juarez in the nineteenth century. In the 1910 revolution this trend was embodied again in the key role played by Emiliano Zapata's largely indigenous peasant-based movement for land reform.

437. (D) The liberal Kerensky regime lasted from the spring to the fall of 1917.

438. (D) In popular consciousness it was the communists who could provide peace, land, and bread—not that peace, land, and bread would provide communism.

439. (D) Old habits did not meet the socialist ideal but were dependable.

440. (B) The Union of Soviet Socialist Republics was made up of these semiautonomous republics.

441. (D) Stalin came to power after the death of Lenin in 1924.

442. (D) Marxism gave subsequent revolutionary movements the explicit goal of a dictatorship of the proletariat.

443. (D) The coal, iron deposits, and timber of Manchuria, as well as the mass markets in China, were an irresistible prize for Japanese imperialists.

444. (B) While the Chinese nationalists never fully suspended offensive operations against communist base areas or suspected communist sympathizers between 1927 and the communist victory in 1949, the period after Japan's all-out invasion of China in 1937 prompted some cessation of hostilities between nationalists and communists in pursuit of the common aim of defeating Japanese aggression.

445. (A) Statement III is untrue of 1920s economic policy, which tended toward a laissez-faire orientation, and hence ruins choices **(B)** and **(C)**.

446. (D) Mounting agricultural overproduction, rising income inequality, weakening purchasing power among the working classes, rampant stock speculation, and irresponsible extension of credit, among other factors, in the 1920s culminated in the stock market crash of 1929. Banks were unable to honor withdrawals and stopped most lending, prompting widespread shutdowns of industrial production. This led to waves of layoffs and rising unemployment that were somewhat ameliorated by FDR's New Deal. Across the industrialized West it was the Second World War and preparation for it that reversed the economic catastrophe of the Great Depression.

447. (B) This advantage of colonial holdings was established during late-nineteenth-century economic downturns.

448. (C) The other nations on the list evolved fascist regimes of some sort.

449. (C) *Lebensraum* translates roughly to "living room." German people had settled in pockets across Slavic Eastern Europe and even into Central Asia by the nineteenth century; in his 1925 book *Mein Kampf* Hitler proposed a campaign to make all these eastern lands a part of a "Greater Germany" where the existing populations would be subjugated and made to serve the interests of the German people.

450. (C) *Mein Kampf* ("My Struggle") was published in 1925 and made Hitler's broad goals for the Third Reich plain for the world to see.

451. (C) With key Italian and German assistance, Franco's fascist forces emerged victorious in the Spanish Civil War; Germany and Japan lost World War II, of course.

452. (B) Statement III ruins choices **(C)** and **(D)** since colonialism ended in the nineteenth century. Both I and II are accurate as the world witnessed the collapse of the Chilean copper industry and the rise of corporatist dictatorial regimes (such as the Vargas regime in Brazil and the Peron regime in Argentina).

453. (D) Fascism involves very tight government supervision of not only the political but also the economic life of a nation. Laissez-faire means just the opposite.

454. (C) Japan's more homogeneous ethnic makeup made events like Kristallnacht (Crystal Night/Night of the Broken Glass), an anti-Jewish movement, a nonissue there.

455. (A) Both regimes are considered to be fascist.

456. (D) Soviet development (as with many developments until recent decades) is not known for environmental concern.

457. (C) *Glasnost* is a Russian term for the economic reforms that allowed for more private ownership, and *perestroika* translates to a new "openness" in politics that allowed for more public criticism of Soviet government and society. Soviet socialism could not survive more than five or six years of these policies.

458. (A) Vast resources inside the USSR, plus access to that of satellite Eastern European nations, make statement III untrue. Since both statements I and II are true, choice **(A)** is best.

459. (D) The Castro dictatorship, by all appearances, is still firmly ensconced in power.

460. (D) This process has accelerated since the dissolution of the Soviet system and the reversion of the entire world economy toward a model with the United States at its center.

461. (A) Vast areas of Africa and Asia will skip the entire "land line" phase of communications development and move right into mobile technologies.

462. (D) Western interests are still central in the world economy but are no longer accompanied by Western flags of colonialism.

463. (C) Major wars in Iraq and Afghanistan have been supplemented by air strikes in Pakistan, Yemen, and Somalia. Most of this action has been taken after September 11 as part of a "War on Terror."

464. (C) While some of the hijackers were United Arab Emirate, Lebanese, and Egyptian, the vast majority of the hijackers were Saudi Arabian.

465. (C) They serve as a preview for the challenges of postcolonial development in a world economy with the West at its economic core.

466. (B) The Bay of Pigs invasion of Cuban exiles was a failure, despite U.S. equipment and air support.

467. (D) Cuba's colonial heritage left it overly dependent on sugar production. The United States imposed a blockade of trade with Cuba soon after 1959, leaving Cuba with few trading partners but the Soviets. Since the 1990 collapse of the USSR, Cuba has struggled for economic growth in the context of this blockade.

468. (D) Cuban socialism has provided choices **(A)** through **(C)**, but Cuban people cannot leave the island easily if they do not like it there.

469. (B) This variant of Catholicism focuses on biblical passages that speak of Jesus' mission to bring justice to this world, and emerged in Latin America in the 1950s and 1960s.

470. (B) The pattern of migration to the cities is, perhaps, surprising to North Americans, but true.

471. (B) This is a unique feature of Mexico in modern Latin American history.

472. (D) This war in the winter of 1989–1990 was launched by the George H. W. Bush administration to remove Manuel Noriega from power in Panama.

473. (A) The days of old-style colonialism were finished by the second half of the twentieth century.

474. (C) Central America, including Mexico, is regarded as part of the North American continent, and NAFTA, short for the North American Free Trade Agreement, was signed in 1994 under the Clinton administration.

475. (C) These events appear in the correct chronology in choice **(C)**, and the experiences of these years shaped subsequent twentieth-century developments in each region of the globe. Before this "Age of Catastrophe," Africa and Asia remained colonized and communists had not seized power anywhere. By 1945 the stage was set for a wave of independence in the colonies and a worldwide confrontation between communist and liberal democratic states, the Cold War, that would last for most of the rest of the century.

476. (A) Considering the broad sweep of the twentieth century, this is the most accurate choice.

477. (D) Political independence for India had to wait for the aftermath of World War II.

478. (B) In South Africa, apartheid lasted until the 1990s.

479. (A) Indian troops as well as African, Australian, New Zealand, Canadian, West Indian, and Irish troops all joined the British side during World War I.

480. (C) The advance of technology in weapons by the early 1900s, particularly the machine gun, resulted in deadlier tactics that necessitated a need for cover by troops.

481. (B) Trench warfare was generally a static form of warfare compared to World War II, which saw blitzkrieg attacks by German forces and surprise attacks by the Japanese.

482. (D) The Morgenthau memoirs remain a powerful indictment against Turkey for its denial of culpability for the genocidal acts committed by the Turkish government during World War I. At the time, the United States was not at war against the Ottomans and had little reason to lie or exaggerate.

483. (C) Rising nationalism led to a push for many groups to establish ethnic states out of the Ottoman Empire. By 1915, groups such as the Greeks, Serbs, Romanians, and Bulgarians had already broken away to form new nations.

484. (A) The poverty and inequality of prerevolutionary Mexicans was the main cause of the revolt and kept it going for 10 long years.

485. (B) Foreign-controlled companies owned by Americans in Mexico or the British in China caused a groundswell of antiforeign sentiment that were one of the main causes of the revolutions in those countries in 1910.

486. (B) In late 1917, Russia was rocked by a second revolution, this time by Bolsheviks, a radical group of communists under their leader Vladimir Lenin.

487. (B) Some historians place 1917 as the start of the Cold War due to the radical economic policies advocated by Russian communists. However, other scholars see the start of the Cold War as events in World War II such as the Yalta Agreement or Red Army liberation of Eastern Europe.

488. (D) The slogan "Peace, Bread and Land" was the Bosheviks' most successful call for support and spoke to the immediate needs of the populace of the Russian empire after three years of world war. The relatively small base of support for communism would become a major challenge to the Bolshevik project.

489. (C) The presence of army generals and navy admirals with tanks, warplanes, and warships show the militant attitudes prevalent among many Japanese people.

490. (A) The rise of fascism in Germany that soon led to the Nazi state saw a glorification of war and was fostered especially among the young through groups such as the Hitler Youth.

491. (D) The World Wars saw the civilian population becoming heavily involved in the war effort in factory work, rallies, and volunteering as well as being subjected to government taxation, rationing, and propaganda. Another notable feature was the increase in civilians beings considered legitimate targets by the enemy.

492. (B) A civil rights movement with both grassroots support and charismatic leaders slowly developed by the mid-1950s and was followed by smaller movements around the world for nonwhite populations.

493. (A) Vietnamese nationalists under Ho Chi Minh hoped to avoid a conflict with both the French and Americans after the war was over. The wording of the document was deliberately chosen for that purpose.

494. (C) The opening of the Declaration with the lines "All men are created equal. They are endowed by their Creator with certain inalienable rights; among these are Life, Liberty, and the pursuit of Happiness" shows a clear influence of the American experience of an independence struggle.

495. (A) Western Cold War priorities tended to paint every conflict in the world as being either for or against communist domination of the world.

496. (D) This United Nations resolution was adopted unanimously by the UN Security Council on November 22, 1967, in the aftermath of the Six-Day War. It has remained the basis for peace talks ever since and was adopted by the Palestinian people.

497. (C) The conflict in the Holy Land has changed over the years from 1967 with no signs of ending but switching from periods of crisis to periods of relative calm.

498. (C) U.S. President John F. Kennedy's famous speech takes strong issue with the idea of a wall to keep East Berliners trapped behind the Iron Curtain and helped it become an iconic symbol of communist oppression.

499. (B) After World War II, many people were alarmed at the rising populations in the developing world. This rehashing of Thomas Malthus's ideas of overpopulation combined with Cold War fears of communism taking hold among poor peoples resulted in attempts to boost agricultural efficiency.

500. (A) The Soviet regime forcibly imposed collective farming, which alienated some prosperous farmers, the so-called *kulaks*. These enemies were then eliminated in the anti-kulak campaigns.

$16.00

LONGWOOD PUBLIC LIBRARY
800 Middle Country Road
Middle Island, NY 11953
(631) 924-6400
longwoodlibrary.org

LIBRARY HOURS

Monday-Friday	9:30 a.m. - 9:00 p.m.
Saturday	9:30 a.m. - 5:00 p.m.
Sunday (Sept-June)	1:00 p.m. - 5:00 p.m.